Enter His Gates

Worship today displays so many wonderful strands spun by the creative hand of God among his people; contemporary and traditional patterns entwine, historical and multi-cultural experiences interlace. But how are we to work with these rich threads? How can personal adoration, corporate praise, form and freedom, the prepared and the spontaneous, be woven together to the glory of God? Here is a book that points the way forward. From her wide experience Ellie Kreider lays biblical foundations and practical directions, which breathe with life and explode with possibilities. Worship is the warp and weft of the Christian community, here is a book fitting it all together.

Noel Moules,
Director, 'Workshop'

Eleanor Kreider is to be congratulated on producing this most stimulating introduction to Christian worship. This is a 'must' for any pastor who wishes to add fresh depth to his services – interesting insights and ideas abound. It is also a 'must' for church members generally, for Eleanor's thesis is that worship leading is not the exclusive prerogative of the pastor. As each chapter ends with a number of searching questions and also some unusual suggestions for action, *Enter His Gates* would form a helpful textbook for Home Groups. This is indeed a paperback with a difference.

Paul Beasley-Murray
Principal, Spurgeon's College

Eleanor Kreider is a remarkable writer, with a deep perception of the Christian worship she is both reporting and commending. She writes not just for pastors, I would judge, but also for any group of Christians planning almost any kind of non-sacramental worship event. She has a straightness of presentation which is easy to follow.

From the point of view of mainstream Christian denominations, and ecumenical studies in worship, her own Mennonite background means that she emphasizes the role of the Word in worship in a way which is both rare and refreshing. The opposite is also true – that the role which she gives to sacraments appears somewhat marginalized, and she is not clear that there is a distinctive Christian eucharist at all. So her chapter on the agape must be viewed as a challenge to dialogue, but her insertion of the scriptural revelation into every feature of worship in all her chapters is simply a joy.

Colin Buchanan

Enter His Gates
Fitting Worship Together

Eleanor Kreider

Marshall Pickering

For my mother
Minnie R. Graber

Marshall Morgan and Scott
Marshall Pickering
34–42 Cleveland Street, London, W1P 5FB, U.K.

Copyright © 1989 E. Kreider

First published in 1989 by Marshall Morgan and Scott Publications Ltd.

Part of the Marshall Pickering Holdings Group

Scripture quotations in this publication are from the Holy Bible, New International Version.
Copyright © 1973, 1978, 1984 International Bible Society. Published by Hodder & Stoughton.

British Library Cataloguing in Publication Data

Kreider, Eleanor
  Enter His gates.
  1. Christian church. Worship
  I. Title
  264

ISBN: 0-551-01942-5

Text set in Times by
Avocet Robinson, Buckingham

Printed in Great Britain by
Cox & Wyman Ltd, Reading, Berkshire

Contents

Introduction

Every day of the year a marvellous mosaic of worship, a sparkling patchwork of prayer, rises in praise of God. 'God, you are the holy one, and we worship you.' Christians in all places – in chapels, in cathedrals, in simple meeting houses, in homes, in school halls, in the open air – express their deepest relationship to the one who has made us. At all times – private morning devotion, evening meetings of small groups, but most of all in Sunday gatherings for corporate worship – Christians pour out their hearts to the one who gives us life.

And yet there is unease. People in every Christian group are aware of inadequacies in their corporate worship. Something, they sense, is incomplete. Things are not all that they could be. Other people, even in the same groups, resist change. Or, if they have changed and grown, they have become self-congratulatory about what they have achieved.

But worship is not about achievement. Worship goes hand in hand with the growth in love to which God calls us. Just as there will always be reasons for unease, there will also always be reasons to go on growing. Always. Until, that is, we join with the elders and martyrs and holy ones from every tribe and every age in heavenly worship. Around the throne in the Holy City we will be worshipping wholly, rightly, in a way that pleases God. But we're not there yet. We all – even those of us who are the most confident about our worship – have much to learn.

What's the Problem?

So what do we need to learn? All of us face the ongoing challenge in our worship of fitting things together. Disparate but essential things. Our worship can be a little like baking a cake which doesn't come out quite right. What's gone wrong? Have we used the wrong kind of flour? Have we forgotten the egg, or put in double the amount of baking powder? Has the cake risen in the oven, but gone flat when it cooled? Our worship cakes sometimes have similar difficulties. Our ingredients don't fuse together. Our worship services, like some of our attempts at baking, can be lumpy or lopsided!

Why does this happen? In this book we will look at various reasons why our corporate worship can be unsatisfying. Three areas will be: our patterns of doing things; our use of the Bible; and our lack of sincerity.

Patterns of doing things Do we spend so much time in praise that we skimp on reflection or confession? Does a long sermon crowd out prayers of intercession? Do we persist in a worship pattern that has 'worked' in the past, in hopes of renewing spontaneity? Do we reject forms because they were imposed on us at school? Do the whims of one man dominate and dictate the balance of our worship?

Bible in worship There is, as James Smart commented, a 'strange silence of the Bible in the church.'[1] Some public worship includes no Bible readings at all. Sometimes pre-set lectionary patterns unduly muffle the Bible's voice. Extempore prayers can be filled with personal clichés rather than with the strong accents of Scripture. But liturgical prayers can hem people in by their biblical though antiquated phrases. And when we do use Scripture in worship we sometimes choose only those parts we like best.

Truth in our worship We sometimes sense a lack of integrity. Are we out of touch with God's character? Are we ignoring the 'world out there'? Or are we unwilling to face the truth about ourselves?

How we answer these questions is important. The answers, in fact, may make us wonder whether we are truly worshipping God. The prophets kept trying to get the message across – God has strong opinions about worship! 'I hate, I despise your religious festivals; I cannot stand your big meetings. Away with the noise of your songs! I will not listen to the music of your organs and guitars. But let justice roll on like a river, righteousness like a never-failing stream!' (Amos 5.21,23–4, slightly modernised). God cannot tolerate phoniness. He wants our worship, but only when it is rooted in a genuine 'desire to do his will' (Ps. 40.8).

1 Are we true to God? Do we direct our worship towards one who is too distant, or too chummy, or who is a caricature of the holy one? Does our theology of the Spirit constrict our worship to expressions and experiences which confine the fire and the power of God to our 'churchy' worship, preventing it from overflowing into the world which God loves? Or are we so insensitive to God-with-us that we fail to hear the risen Christ among us, healing us and calling us to practical, daily discipleship?

2 Are we true to our world? Do we forget that God created, delights in, and loves the world, and that he intends to redeem it? Our lives are intertwined with the people in everyday life – do we bring their concerns into our worship? How about politics – matters of peace and justice, health and compassion? Jesus, like the Old Testament prophets, cared about these things. Can we truly follow Jesus, can we be faithful disciples and loving neighbours, if these concerns are quarantined out of our worship?

3 Are we true to ourselves? Do we play games with ourselves – and each other? Do we forget that God loves us, and knows all our distinctive ways? Do we need a truer understanding of ourselves and a deeper reception of God's acceptance? The integrity of our praise depends on this. What did Paul mean when he urged the Romans, 'Accept one another, then, just as Christ accepted you, in order to bring praise to God' (Romans 15.7)?

Fitting Worship Together

What a list of questions! Through the Holy Spirit, God keeps nudging us towards a fuller integration of worship and life that he desires for us. God wants to lead us in the task of fitting worship together.

Fitting Our worship needs to be 'fitting' in another sense, too. Worship which should be appropriate to the size of congregation and to the shape of the space. Paul tells early Christians to do everything 'in a fitting and orderly way' (I Cor. 14.40). Our forms, too, must suit the people we are. They must be comprehensible to visitors, they must fit the local surroundings, and they must be flexible enough to grow and develop.

Worship Worship! This word, when defined biblically, will prove to be a large and life-embracing word. We cannot be content with a definition in which, too simply, 'worship' = praise. Biblical worship happens when we as individuals and as communities of faith communicate with the holy and loving God who made us. It involves not only our personal lives, but also our economic and social lives. Worship engages our emotions, our minds, our desires. Through it we listen to and obey God. All our lives are bound up in worship that is 'in spirit and in truth' (John 4.24).

10

Together   It's not a matter for individuals, is it? The Bible's vision is for corporate worship in which everyone takes part. It can't be done by a few 'professionals' who perform acts of worship on our behalf. And we can't really do it alone. God draws differing people together in the unity that is his will for us.

All Christian traditions face the challenge of fitting worship together. And all of us can learn from other Christian traditions if we are open to each other. We Christians need each other.

I am intensely aware of this. I was born in India (where my parents were Mennonite missionaries) and raised in the United States. My parents were conscious of their Anabaptist heritage, and passed on this awareness to their children. The heritage was of a church that is both suffering and familial, in the radical reformation tradition. As an adult, I chose to affirm this heritage and to live within it. I continue to rejoice in its particular strengths of earthiness and practical piety.

But for all the strengths of my own tradition, I have learned much from others. I have been enriched by the Anglican tradition through several years of regular worship in parish churches. I have known the rekindling of fervour and praise in charismatic worship. Among Quaker friends and Christian contemplatives I have learned to listen to God through corporate silence. And, strange though this may seem, I have been inspired – and given a vision – by academic study: the worship in the early church, I believe, offers new and compelling insights.

By training, a musician, and by experience, a teacher, I approach worship with an artist's eye and a desire to analyse and improve. Without doubt, the threshing floor of my ideas on worship has been conversation with my husband, Alan. Two people – Andrew Kreider and Gwen Groff – have helped me

11

greatly with clarity of thought and expression. But I have also experienced much in my congregation. It is here, in the London Mennonite Fellowship, recently renamed the Wood Green Mennonite Church, in north London, that I have received – and been allowed to give – the most.

Nowhere, not even in the early church, have Christians completely 'fitted worship together'. There has never been a perfect church. So we Christians need each other. We can pray and work for forms of worship that will be integrated and whole. Whatever our tradition, it is possible for worship to be more 'together', more biblical, and more Jesus-centred.

1: Truth in Worship

A. True to God

We Worship a Personal God

Worship is personal. Of course, it's theological, too, and social and practical. It can be earthy, and sometimes mysterious and frightening. But most of all, worship is a relationship, something that goes on between persons, between us and God.

To begin a relationship, we need to meet. So where do we meet God? If we are willing to see it, we can recognise God's hand at every turn: in the beauty of a bright yellow pansy, in the provision and safety of our everyday life, in music, in friendship, or in the pleasure of a straight row of onion plants in the garden. And we can say to each other, 'Isn't that just like God! It's just what he would do!'

'Isn't that just like him! It's exactly what you'd expect from Jim.' How often we use these words in describing a person we know well. Jim, so quick to make visitors feel at home, offers them a drink, a cushion, a game. Always thinking ahead, wanting to help. His impulses, his actions, spell out his character.

And that's how it is with God. We read his character by his actions. In the Bible we find out what he is like by what he has done through human history. The Bible is history. The Bible is story. And the story-line through the whole Bible is about God forming a people whom he has liberated from oppression, loved and nurtured. It is a story of relationships, of promise and faithfulness, of carelessness and treachery, of tears and joys. Through the Bible story we learn that though

God's people so often spurned his love, God has still looked after them as he pursues his *big idea* of bringing it all right in the end – 'to bring all things in heaven and on earth together under one head, even Christ' (Eph. 1.10). The climax of the Bible story is in Jesus, who in human personality showed who God is, and showed us how to be in relationship with God the Father. We learn to know God and to form a relationship with God through the Bible story, and most vividly, through Jesus.[2]

Worship is what we call our side of the relationship. But first we must meet God, learn to recognise him. Psalm 145 reminds us how to do this. It tells us what God is like, what he does, and who he is in relation to history and to his creation. God is a God of 'mighty acts' and 'wonderful works' (Ps. 145.4–5). The adjectives of this psalm are eloquent: God is gracious, merciful, good, compassionate, faithful, tender, just and kind. The verbs are just as powerful: God gives, satisfies, fulfils the desires of every living thing. He hears, saves and preserves. These are all personal words about an active God. They describe the character of God, learned and known through his interventions in history and his dealings with his people.

And how do we respond to our God? The action words in Psalm 145 put it so well: we extol, bless, praise, laud, declare the actions, meditate, proclaim, pour forth his fame, sing aloud, give thanks, tell, make known his goodness. This list of responses is the beginning of a definition of worship. Worship is our total personal response, individually and together as God's people, to our God.

'Glorious splendour', transcendence, omnipotence, power, beauty, otherness. These are God words, too. They remind us that our God is bigger, more, beyond our words and our experience. But God communicates best to us through his story, through his actions. That's why the Bible is primarily a history book.

So God is the creator. God is the liberator, setting free captives and oppressed people. God is involved with our human life. God is re-creator, too, with a plan for the renewal of creation, 'a new heaven and a new earth, the home of justice' (II Pet. 3.13). God has a huge design – world historical and cosmic in scope. And he puts us into it to be his co-workers.

Why worship? Why recognise and respond to God? Because we are mysteriously made for that response. It is in us to look for God. 'Seek me and live!' says God (Amos 5.4). Worship is about life, our personal life in God, and our life together under God's loving reign.

True Worship Reflects Who God Is
All through Scripture we see that God wanted to relate to a people, not just to individuals. From the beginning of the story, worship was social. Worship was the meeting point, the relationship of a people with their God. It is still that way. In true worship we will catch the vision of God's character, and then reflect his concerns and purposes.

God's people sometimes get it terribly wrong. In Isaiah Chapter 1, God thunders at them, 'Who asked you to trample my courts? I cannot bear your evil assemblies. They have become a burden to me. When you spread out your hands in prayer, I will hide my eyes from you. Even if you offer many prayers, I will not listen. Your hands are full of blood' (Isa. 1.12–5).

Why was God so angry? The people had blood on their hands. They had done evil. Their society was oppressive and unjust. Their top people were taking advantage of the weak and defenceless (Isa. 1.16–7).

This was the way of death. So the people who chose it could have no relationship with the God of life. What they called worship was, in fact, non-worship. In God's eyes their beautiful ceremonies were foul, rotten play-acts. As long as the people denied God's character, as long as they forgot God's liberating actions and ignored

15

his concerns for justice and compassion, they could not worship him.

This does not mean that God wanted them to be perfect before he would accept their worship. On their own they could never build a perfect society. But since God reads the intentions of the heart, he did require that the people remember his love and align themselves with his concerns. If they refused to do so God would neither listen nor respond to them.

'Learn to do right! Seek justice, encourage the oppressed. Defend the cause of the fatherless, plead the cause of the widow' (Isa. 1.17). What will honour God? 'The Lord will be exalted by justice' (Isa. 5.16). In these passages Isaiah points the way back to true worship. When the nation's life reflects God's concerns, God will hear their prayers. Then the people can worship him in truth.

In Jeremiah's time the people, regardless of the injustices in society, clung to worship services which they believed were a source of security. 'The temple of the Lord, the temple of the Lord', they chanted (Jer. 7.4). God was not pleased. His perspective was different from theirs, and he severely warned them of necessary judgment. God's word through Jeremiah spelled out the conditions for life, and for true worship. Apart from these conditions, the people could never find God's favour.

'If you really change your ways and your actions and deal with each other justly, if you do not oppress the alien, the fatherless or the widow and do not shed innocent blood in this place and if you do not follow other gods to your own harm, then I will let you live in this place' (Jer. 7.3–7). 'Will you steal and murder, commit adultery and perjury, burn incense to Baal and follow other gods you have not known, and then come and stand before me in this house which bears my Name and say "We are safe" – safe to do these detestable things? Has this house, which bears my

16

Name, become a den of robbers to you?' (Jer. 7.9–11).

First do justice, and then come to worship. Care for the weak, and then come to worship. Have mercy, and then come to worship. In our Bible, and in our world, too, these things belong together! The prophets show us that they must not be pulled apart. If they are, if our corporate acts do not reflect our God's character, his actions, and his concerns, we may call it 'worship,' but it will be something else.

Jesus, the Centre Point

Jesus came as the last and greatest in the line of the prophets. Supremely, he conveyed what God is like, what God's concerns are. Jesus fits together for us how human life can be in tune with God. He shows the way to true communication with God, the way to true worship. In God's story Jesus is unique. He was God's Son, his direct intervention, his perfect revelation.

Jesus is the centre point of history. In our lifelong relationship with God, we have been given Jesus as the Way, the Truth and the Life (John 14.6). Jesus shows us what God is like, what God cares about. Through Jesus' actions and concerns God has shown the way of new creation, breaking into the present and pointing to the goal of history – the new city, the new earth and new heaven.

But Jesus is our human brother, too. He knew the frustrations and difficulties, the testing and the joys of human life. He showed the way to whole, true human relationships. And he invited his disciples into an intimate relationship with Abba, the heavenly Father.

Jesus lived the beatitude life of humility, self-abasement and suffering. He spoke and he acted. He prayed and he worshipped. He invited individuals – and he invites us – to follow in his steps. We can learn to worship from Jesus, our best teacher, if we walk and live in his way.

How puzzling, then, that Christian worship so often

avoids Jesus. What other religion in the world, what followers of a holy guru, have so neglected the private and public repetitions of their leader's teachings?

According to the Gospel, Jesus came preaching the kingdom of God. He told stories to illustrate what that reign of God means. His actions of power, reconciliation and mercy demonstrated it. We know that God's kingdom was of paramount importance to Jesus. So why doesn't Jesus' emphasis more often become our emphasis? In our services and liturgies do we pray 'prayers of the kingdom'?

In Luke Chapter 4, verses 18 and 19, Jesus stated the manifesto of his ministry. This was the definition of his life's calling. 'Good news for the poor . . . release to the captives . . . recovery of sight . . . freedom for the oppressed . . . proclaiming the year of the Lord's favour.' Should not these phrases and ideas be like gold nuggets in every service of Christian worship?

It is a loss that Christians have not followed the Jewish disciplines of memorising the teachings of the rabbis. Except for the Lord's Prayer, Jesus' own words are virtually absent as corporate or choric parts of public Christian worship. Can we repeat the Beatitudes by heart? If we cannot, does this say something about their importance to us? Too often we use Jesus' words as points of departure instead of focusing directly upon them. If we were to make the stories and words of Jesus central to our worship, it could be immeasurably deepened. We could expose our lives more often and more fully to the Gospel.

Living and worshipping for several months with the sisters in the Communauté de Grandchamp, I saw a remarkable example of such integration. Conscious awareness of the person and teachings of Jesus marked the daily life of the community. In a service every evening we heard the Gospel reading for the following day. We heard it again in the morning, and portions of the same passage once more at noon. After hearing the same Gospel passage several times, we could return to it, internally, throughout the day, allowing its meanings to flower.

But the sisters emphasised that we should focus on more than the words of Jesus and their potential meanings. It was important to visualise Jesus actually saying and doing the things we were hearing in the Gospel. Everyone taking part in the daily worship was united because we carried with us similar internal words and images from the Gospel readings. Unity through worship and prayer were of prime importance to the sisters. Jesus himself stood at the very centre of that unity.

Jesus' healing ministry was central to his vocation. It was an expression of God's love, a sign of God's kingdom. Even from the earliest centuries of the Church, healing prayers have had only a small place in Christian corporate worship. But at last, in our own day, some churches are learning to include this ministry, following Jesus' emphasis, in or adjacent to public worship.

By word and by example, Jesus taught us about worship. We can still follow him, learning to worship in spirit and in truth. He told us it is not enough to say, 'Lord, Lord, didn't we prophesy in your name? Lord, Lord, didn't we cast out demons in your name, and perform many miracles?' Jesus asks for more than words. We must 'do the will of [his] Father who is in heaven' (Matt. 7.21). Our worship, being true to Jesus, will reflect Jesus. His words, his communion with the Father, his passion to announce God's kingdom, his willingness to pray and to heal – all these will characterise our worship.

Holy Spirit, the Communicator
It seems such an impossibly big order, trying to talk and live as Jesus did, and to worship in spirit and in truth. Jesus knew that it would be impossible for his disciples,

left to their own devices. But he had a wonderful secret for them. Something was to happen that would make all the difference. He told them (John 14.16) that he would pray to the Father and that they would receive the Spirit of truth and strength for all their needs. This Spirit would be *with* them, *in* them, *among* them.

Jesus promised, 'The Holy Spirit . . . will teach you all things and will remind you of everything I have said to you' (John 14.26). But how often the person and words of Jesus get shoved out of our worship. 'When the Spirit comes, he will guide you into all truth' (John 16.13). But all too often our worship is untrue to God, the world and ourselves. 'Where the Spirit is, there is freedom' (II Cor. 3.17). But sometimes people get squashed in worship, dominated by the exercise of 'lordship' by leaders who are not servants. Where the spirit is, there is 'justice, peace and joy' (Romans 14.17). Tragically, we have all experienced worship which tries to grow in the rocky ground of oppression, fear, laziness or pride.

The presence of the Holy Spirit makes all the difference in our worship. The Holy Spirit allows Jesus' words to come alive, he changes our hearts and energises our wills. The Holy Spirit can enliven our forms of worship to enable joy and spontaneity. The Holy Spirit breaks through human limitations, and links us with God. And somehow when this happens, our worship more faithfully reflects God's concerns. It displays the strong and loving characteristics of Jesus. The Holy Spirit leads us into worship that rings true.

For Thought and Action

What is God like? Search through the Bible, keep a list of God's characteristics and concerns.

Would a visitor recognise these characteristics reflected faithfully in your church's worship?

How can you enlarge your grasp of healing prayers, and

include them in (alongside) public worship?

How can silence, time to listen to the Holy Spirit, find a place in worship?

Judge worship by its fruit in life of church:
mercy, justice, healing, inclusion of outsiders, shalom.

Is Jesus regularly referred to and quoted in worship?

How is Jesus most often described – as servant, reigning in majesty, as friend, saviour?

How can we help ourselves to memorise Jesus' words?

Practise re-telling, re-casting Jesus' stories in worship.

Write prayers, benedictions which include Jesus' words.

Make posters, banners, other visual reminders of God's character, Jesus' life, the Holy Spirit's power.

B. True to the World

Worship and the World — Any Connections?
'All I want is my privacy and anonymity in the presence of God. The church no longer provides a setting for concentrated and detached worship.'[3]

A place for individual 'detached worship' is the plea of this *Church Times* correspondent. Many Christians feel this way, and are offended by attempts to introduce changes such as passing the peace. That this view contradicts New Testament teaching about corporate prayer and worship seems to make little difference. Holy remove is exactly what many Western Christians want worship to be.

By looking into our history we can see how this individualised understanding of worship developed. The Christian religion has, in every period and place, taken on a particular emphasis according to the culture of the newly Christianised people. These changing emphases have been expressed in their worship.[4]

For example, when Christianity stopped being a sect within the Jewish religion and spread into the Roman

Empire, it took on the distinct philosophic, rational hue of the prevalent Greek culture. Right ways of thinking and proper statements of belief became important to Christians. Early Jewish Christians probably would have been puzzled or uncomfortable with the 'new' emphasis. Disputes over dogma loomed over Church life, so it is not surprising that during this period credal formulations were increasingly important in worship. Right belief, devoutly stated, became a foundation of worship.

Christians in the first centuries, in spite of the world-embracing vision of their faith, were forced by legal restriction to worship in private. And sometimes persecution forced them to hide their worship from the world. Such 'private' Christian worship reflected the ethos and relationships possible in their intimate groupings. The earliest Christian cells were small groups of people who knew each other by name. Each one knew the exact circumstances of life of the other members. Intimate prayers and a family atmosphere of worship were a natural expression of the Church in this era.[5]

The following centuries saw Christianity conquer and adapt to new cultures, although in some areas such as North Africa, where it had been deeply rooted, it was wiped out by Islam. In each era, the worship patterns adapted too, and reflected the philosophical, social and economic realities of the populations.

In Europe, Christianity took on some of the characteristics of tribal religion in that it adapted to the cultures of the people. Whole nations of people could be 'made Christian' by the decision of the chief or prince – backed up by force.[6] Unimaginable changes in worship were necessary to accommodate the crowds of uninstructed converts in new church buildings. These Europeans were not Greek philosophers, and had to be reached through ways other than argument of right belief. People who could not read books could be taught to 'read' sculpture and stained glass. Architecture and music joined with other visual and dramatic elements to express faith in forms of worship never known before. Christians of these centuries may have found incomprehensible our question about whether worship is connected to the world. Politics, religion and economics were all part of one fabric of life on this side of the final judgment.

For Christians in the Western European tradition, one of the most significant changes was the incorporation of the conviction that everyone is personally accountable. Belief and rules for life became less subject to tribal or kinship patterns. Each person had to make decisions and had to take the eternal consequences of those decisions. The concept of individualism has permeated Western Christian worship. The result is that we are now caught in traditions of intensely personalised and individualised piety. One of the effects is the isolation which many worshippers experience. Focusing on their individual relationships to God, they lose a sense of connection with others and with the world beyond their own preoccupations.

So we see that in various historical periods we can find new elements in the worship of the 'new' Christianity. The new aspects have affected every area of the church's life – its dogmas, its ethos, its structures, its prayer and its public worship. When we observe worship patterns we can be a bit like a doctor looking into the human eyeball for signs of hidden conditions. In a church's worship there are clues to its overall health.

One of the notable characteristics of Christian worship in our time is its separation from the world. Extreme individualisation of belief and piety has limited the scope of our prayers and reduced engagement with the harsh and fallen world.

It is hard for us to realise how isolated from the world we really are. How do our churchy activities, our

Christian language and our worship appear to non-Christians? Perhaps it is similar to the way I feel about the local betting shop. I walk past it, notice its name and the window decorations. But I have only vague ideas about what goes on inside. It looks dark and unappealing to me. But I'm not much bothered one way or another about it.

What goes on in the betting shop has as much relevance to me as Christian worship does to many people who pass by the church buildings in the course of their daily routines. The buildings are pleasant enough to look at, but what happens inside is a mystery, and not a very compelling one at that. Most people don't give it a second thought.

Cosmos and Worship

The Bible challenges our double-life. Nowhere in Scripture is there a rationale for a split between worship and world. The law, the prophets, the writings, Jesus and the apostles – all summon us to confront the world and to engage it in worship.

'Cosmos', the Greek word for world in the New Testament, literally means 'order'. God designed and created the world (cosmos) in elaborate, intricate order. Even after evil entered and disordered his good creation, God loved the cosmos (John 3.16). The Bible story is about God's actions in re-ordering and re-creating the world that he loves.

At its best, the worship of Israel, God's chosen people, was a way to connect the obedient lives of the people with the world in which they lived. According to God's call, Israel was to be a sign and an instrument of the re-creation and healing of the world. And Israel's worship was to be a rallying point for the entire world. God's house is to be 'a house of prayer for all nations' (Isa. 56.7). 'Many nations will stream to God's mountain and learn his ways' (Mic. 4.2). The psalms depict a time, surely coming, when all creation will gather

24

around his throne to worship Yahweh, the 'king above all gods'. Yahweh's plan is to re-create his creation; he calls all of creation into the order and peace which he intended in the beginning. Cosmic worship will be the ultimate festival of 'creation healed'.[7]

Telling the Story

The worship of Israel centred around telling and re-telling the story of Yahweh's acts in liberating and sustaining his people. He was the one who created, who watched, who listened and liberated. He gave his people the Torah; he kept covenant with them; he protected them and provided for them. By drama and story, by symbol and pilgrimage, the people recounted and celebrated Yahweh in their worship. They remembered that he, who was wholly other, was also a *worldly* God.

Jesus Makes the Connection

So it's not surprising that Jesus was committed to keeping worship and the world connected. As we 'go to church' with him, we can see how passionate was his commitment to the connection. Following him into worship, we might become uneasy. It could even be a bit dangerous. We will observe him incensed with just anger; we will watch him disturbing divine services; and we will find the religious establishment turning on him. What had gone so wrong with worship that Jesus had to 'cleanse the temple'?

As Mark tells the story, when Jesus came to the temple he found 'the world' in full operation, profiteering by exchanging money into temple currency and selling birds and animals for temple sacrifices. These temple businessmen, formerly selling in market areas near the temple, had pushed their way inside the temple precincts, thereby making more money at the expense of poor people. They boldly set up their enterprises within the Court of the Gentiles, the very space intended for the non-Jewish adherents to pray and worship. How were the nations to come to God if their area of the temple had been taken over by commercial interests?

Jesus was outraged at the sight. In the temple the world was present all right, in the guise of rampant commercialism. But the world that God loves and wants to redeem – the enemies, the outsiders, the nations – had been excluded. The temple, Jesus concluded, had been desecrated. 'My house will be called a house of prayer for all nations. But you have made it a den of robbers' (Mark 11.17). No wonder he began to brandish a whip, sending coins rolling and turtle doves flapping (John 2.15). No wonder that the temple authorities 'began looking for a way to kill him' (Mark 11.18)!

Jesus was dangerous. His actions demonstrated that worship which isn't explicitly conscious of the world becomes worldly in more insidious ways!

Christian worship and cosmos belong together. The best in our biblical and historical past tells us that they do. But we Christians have long traditions of sealing worship off from the world. We perceive the world as simply evil. Or, more often, as simply secular – the area where religion does not apply.[8] We repeat the truisms that the world is 'fallen' and the order disordered. All too often we Christians have thought that mentioning our involvement in the world in the sacred space of Sunday worship will defile our services. Economics, social work, or architecture mentioned in our church services? Heaven forbid! Shock horror!

'We don't want politics in our worship. Politics are for television. Worship is for the church. Don't mix them up.' How familiar! When we bring our world into our worship, things heat up. Sermons and prayers get controversial. We offend each other. Worship no longer feels peaceful.

But we are more worldly than we know. If we try to

keep the world out of worship, it will come in anyhow. We bring our world with us. The apostle Paul saw this happening in the Corinthian church (I Cor. 11). The Christians in Corinth were very spiritual. They celebrated the Lord's Supper; they even excercised spiritual gifts in their meetings. But they did not do 'the will of the Father in heaven'. They, in effect, said, 'Lord, Lord' (Matt. 7.21), but in their services they accentuated the difference between rich and poor. The rich were insensitive. The poor were humiliated. And as a result, Paul told them, 'When you come together, it is not the Lord's Supper that you are eating' (I Cor. 11.20). From his perspective, their worship, distorted by economic inequality, was 'doing more harm than good' (I Cor. 11.17). What an indictment!

Let us take Paul's words to heart. If, when we come to the Lord's table, we don't recognise the economic divisions among us, we too, are in danger of doing more harm than good.

Whose supper are we celebrating? If it is truly the Lord's supper, let's remember who else he has invited there. Jesus said that there will be surprising people at the feast; tax-collectors and sinners and people coming 'from east and west, from north and south. They will take their places at the feast in the kingdom of God' (Luke 13.29). We, too, are invited to eat the meal, the sign of God's immense generosity, in the presence of the world's marginal and poor people. The world is invited to the table of the kingdom!

'But politics and worldly concerns in our worship will mar the unity of our church!' Unity which isn't based on truth is bogus. Unity based on selective blindness to the world induces hard-heartedness in the Church. It means ignoring Jesus' engagement with the disordered world. It means refusing to do our 'work' of worship and intercession for the world. It is a cheap unity that bars the real concerns of the world from our worship.

This must be made practical. Later in the book we

will explore some ways to express these concerns through prayers of intercession, confessions and communion services.

Christians are called to be a 'royal priesthood' (I Pet. 2.9). This is not simply a calling to serve other like-minded people. This priesthood is for the world. Through our intercession we can bring before God the world he loves. Equally, through our worship we can convey God's love and grace to an anguished world.

For Thought and Action

In what ways do worldly philosophies (e.g., separation of spiritual and material) and values (e.g., time is money) influence our worship?

Does our worship explicitly challenge worldly values (e.g., giving priority to concerns of the weak)?

How does our worship show that we are serious about our human responsibility to take care of the created world? Do we work and pray for 'creation healed'?

Does fear of conflict (e.g., over politics, peace or social issues) prevent unity in praying in public worship for 'cosmos healed'? How can the fears be overcome, the conflicts resolved?

Notice specific points (e.g., intercessions, testimonies, benedictions) where you can make connections between worship and the realities of the everyday world.

C. True to Ourselves

The little bird snuggles down into its nest, only a bright eye keeping watch. She has found a safe niche in a carved fold of the altar. The psalmist evokes a picture of security and peace, an ideal home for fledgeling young.

'Oh, the happiness, the peace, the wholeness of

those who live in the house of God!' the poet exclaims. 'They are continually praising God' (Ps. 84.4). Being secure and at peace, being ourselves, we can be at home with God. And there we can wholeheartedly praise him. It is wonderful to feel completely at ease in worship, completely at home. For that to happen, we must be willing to take risks. We must be willing to know ourselves; we must be willing to be known by God.

The Truth about Ourselves

> Surely you desire truth in the inner parts;
> Teach me wisdom in the inmost place (Ps. 51.6).

Psalm 51, the best-loved 'penitential' psalm, guides us through searing grief and despair into the assurance of God's forgiveness and acceptance. The psalmist tells us that the path to joy and gladness leads by way of a contrite spirit (v. 17). But he starts down that path in learning to know the truth about himself, bringing God's wisdom to bear on his most secret inner being (v. 6). Renewed in his spirit, the poet can joyfully exclaim: 'My tongue will sing of your justice. O Lord, open my lips, and my mouth will declare your praise' (vv. 13–4).

The psalmist's path to worship is our path as well. There may be much inside ourselves which we don't understand, things we blush to remember. When we prepare to meet God, we come to him as wholly and truly as we can. We offer God our memories of his faithfulness in our past, and our commitment to walk in the way of Jesus. But we offer him what we don't understand of ourselves as well, trusting him to receive us in grace and love.

Accepting the Truth about Each Other

God has made us different from each other. But who we are deeply affects our individual spiritual expressions. Some of us are outgoing and love to talk,

29

some enjoy quiet, some like being in large groups, and some don't. It is obvious that these preferences will affect how we worship. In every group gathered for worship there will be a great variety of people. How do they expect to participate? What do they hope to receive from the worship? How will they respond to words, music, drama, visual aids or silence? What we expect and how we respond are not necessarily good or bad. Our differences are, after all, evidence of God's amazing virtuosity in creation.[9]

Who comes to Worship?

Not only for those who plan worship, but also for all who participate, is it useful to notice and understand the effects of differences in personality types within the congregation. We can become more patient with our various ways of listening, learning, responding and praying together. The following anecdote will illustrate some of the variety in personality types seen in every congregation.

Crash! Shattering, shimmering waves of bronze enveloped the normally staid congregation that Sunday morning. 'Praise the Lord with resounding cymbals!' Surely the poet himself never heard such a lively rendition of Psalm 150!

'They've done it again,' muttered Ian. 'That worship committee has found a novel way to open the service.' The young percussion player was delighted. He had been asked to do something unique in the church service. Behind the hidden cymbals in the balcony, he thoroughly enjoyed the jumps and starts of the faithful as he 'called them to worship'.

Ian protested. He didn't feel 'called to worship'. Every Sunday morning unexpected things kept happening. One week it was choral reading, the next it was children bearing banners, and now these insufferable cymbals. Was any of it necessary? Ian had been a member at this church for years. He never missed a Sunday. Every week he and his wife sat in the same place, just to the front of the second window on the right. They made a point of arriving in good time, so that he could look up the Bible readings and get the hymn numbers ready. Their minister led a good service, never preached too long, and dismissed them on time. This was a good church for Ian. But lately all these disturbing innovations, the work of a new-fangled worship committee, were putting Ian off. He'd best go and have a word with the minister.

Every church has its Ian. He is like a barometer for those who plan details for the services. 'Can we get this past Ian?' they wonder as they plan the children's banner procession for Pentecost. How sad that Ian's pearly qualities – his faithfulness, his devoted (if dogged) attendance at all church events, his careful work on church finances – are often undervalued. Instead he is almost feared. He is seen as a hindrance, a block to progress.

Yes, every church has its Ian. But every church has its Ed, too. As we press our ear to the keyhole of the minister's office, we hear Ed's voice booming out: 'Say, I liked the way you read the notices right at the beginning of the service yesterday. What a surprise! That bit about the mystery benefit supper made everyone look around at each other and smile. That was good. It made us feel we belonged together. Looking into each other's faces is so much better than just looking at the backs of people's heads. It was a good way to begin the service, sort of personal for a change. Much better than so much quiet. The worship committee is doing a good job with some new ideas, and they keep us on our toes.'

But the minister was smiling inwardly as he recalled another member, Irene's, comments after the same service. She had so much appreciated the pause for quiet after the Gospel reading. So often the pace was

31

too fast for her, she had said. This week she had enjoyed closing her eyes and visualising Jesus as he had been portrayed in the reading, speaking kindly to the centurion and graciously healing his servant. Irene had continued hesitantly, 'I don't like to criticise, but I must confess that I found it jarring to have the notices at the beginning of the service.' She was used to coming in and sitting quietly before the service, reading the Scripture for the day, and inwardly preparing herself for the worship.

If all members were like Ian, or all like Irene, there would be little call for worship committees. Such committees are usually formed of people who are eager to stretch the established forms of their church's worship patterns, to add new artistic expressions, to explore variety, to try new possibilities. Sometimes a church, alarmed by the polarity caused by too much innovation, will appoint an Ian or an Irene to the committee to keep the Eds under control. A familiar syndrome of conflict, or, sometimes, paralysis, results. Must this happen? Is there a way to understand, to cope with these apparently irreconcilable poles?

The obvious reason for the conflict is the immense variety in human personality present in every social group. We can observe the same fundamental problems at our workplaces, at school, and in our families. Some of us function best in a clear structure, with well-defined expectations, with routines. Others of us find such structures inhibiting, and we long for a chance to try a new way, to improve, to tinker with accepted patterns. Between these poles of attitudes about forms come all the rest of us, with our individual combinations of preferences in approaching decisions, in establishing relationships, in coping with changes in our lives.

Our personality types deeply affect our individual spiritual expression as well as our corporate religious life. For example, the methodical, careful person may value regular, quiet devotions in her prayer life, and experience God in an intensely personal relationship. Such a person's preferences in public worship are not hard to predict. She will like established patterns, ones that don't put unexpected demands upon her. She will value times for silent reflection.

On the other hand, an extrovert may experience God most vividly in the presence of others. He may find that prayer can be acted out in helping his neighbour. Drawing his energy from sources outside himself, he enjoys praying in groups, and will always be open to trying new ideas in corporate worship.

Knowing Ourselves, Honouring Each Other

There is great scope for deepening our understanding and appreciation of each other by coming to terms with the basic differences in our individual ways of reaching out and responding to God. It is not a matter of this person or that having a good or bad way of worshipping. It's not that there are worst and best ways of praying. The important thing is to approach with caution and humility the variety of human personalities and to make a place for each person present to enter into the corporate worship.

If first we know and accept ourselves, we are then able to accept each other, varied as we are. 'Let love be sincere (genuine)', says Paul. 'Think of yourselves with sober judgement . . .' 'honour one another above yourselves' (Romans 12.3,9,10).

Variety Programme or Dominant Personality?

A worshipping congregation is always made up of a marvellous variety of people. This is obvious! But what difference does it make in the way we approach worship, the way we plan for it and the way we experience it?

Attempting to cope with the variety of people in the congregation, some churches try to achieve balance by providing something for all 'interests'. One church has a rule that each of its two hymn books must be used equally. Eight minutes of Watts/Wesley counterbalances eight minutes of guitar choruses. Another church has three Bible readings in each service. Readers are chosen by category: one man, one woman, one person under twenty. Ten minutes for the children's story, ten minutes for intercessions.

All too often this approach turns worship into a 'formula' variety programme. Perhaps an unconscious model is the popular magazine, where nothing in the balance of content is left to chance or inspiration. Fashion, fiction, food, family, features: all is expertly designed to attract and hold a precisely predicted reader.

Another approach results in the worship itself having a dominant 'personality'. Sometimes this is because a particular person always leads the worship. Perhaps the congregation is propelled into a stream of singing or responses by a continuous flow of exuberance from the leader up front. Perhaps the worship is predictably and completely uniform in following a set form. A church with a dominant style in worship, or with a characteristic personality of worship, will become self-selecting in its members. Those who cannot easily move into the particular way of doing things will simply go elsewhere.

A Church's Personality — towards Maturity

A church, just as an individual, can be on the path towards maturity. The personality of a church will express this growing maturity in its corporate worship. Learning, changing and growing – a church's worship will reflect the general health and vigour of other aspects of the congregation's life.

Each of us goes through periods of change. We can be strengthened through our pain. We can learn through our failures, develop our ideas and find help in the counsel of others. The movement towards maturity

34

is marked by vigilance and discrimination, by integration and discipline. As maturing people, we welcome insight and deepen our ability to accept the validity of experiences and expression other than our own.

In the same ways that a person develops, a church can increase maturity. This requires self-understanding. The Church needs to respect its own history and seek out the very best expressions of its tradition. The Church must curb the tendency to indulge its 'typical' features. That indulgence results in the Church becoming a caricature of its better self.

Whatever the tendency of a particular tradition – whether it is a love affair with words, a super-personal atmosphere, a grand family reunion fellowship style, or an aesthetic 'trip' – each church must draw on the best of its tradition without allowing the tendencies to become crippling.

But how do we know the difference between drawing on the tradition and developing crippling limps? I can illustrate this by my own church. Characteristic of Mennonite churches is the earthy emphasis on faith being validated in everyday life. For Mennonites, business ethics, care of the earth and family relationships must reflect the words of worship and prayer. People within the church are known and are willing to be known. The sense of being an interdependent people is a positive feature of the Mennonite tradition.

If we overplay communalism, however, we may miss other important aspects of faith and worship. A caricatured Mennonite worship, for example, would not foster a sense of the awe and separateness of God, his majestic and cosmic kingdom. Fellowship, the horizontal aspects within corporate worship and prayer, would outbalance other equally important factors.

Jesus was aware of the kind of balancing act that we need in our piety and in our worship: '. . . these you

35

ought to have done, without neglecting the others'
(Matt. 23.23).

Vigilance and self-awareness, discipline and integration – all these qualities exercised in the love described in I Corinthians, chapter 13 will produce a worshipping church of maturity and grace. Its worship will honour God, and build up the fellowship.

For Thought and Action

Does your worship help you to accept the truth about yourselves – weakness, strengths and differences?

Try to listen effectively to each other's experience in worship. Can you develop flexibility in forms and content in light of who's there in worship?

Do you believe that a worship service can serve each other as well as God? Can you consciously serve the weakest ones – the deaf, the young, the old, the distressed?

Can you encourage and build each other up in the ways you worship? Can you say 'thank you' and 'it was helpful' more frequently to those who participate?

Try to balance elements in each service so that all types of people can easily respond to at least one aspect: a challenge to action, a quiet reflective moment, an activity, something visual, some linear thinking, creative art forms.

Draw on your church's 'family history' – its tradition: tell the stories, value the strengths, recapture positive, old forms (if any), supplement weaknesses in your church tradition with insights from others.

2: Design in Worship

A. It's How We Do It

Punch Press

My niece worked nights in a small factory, operating a vicious machine that meticulously punched holes in steel plates. Her hands were fastened into slings which automatically flung them to safety each time the punch came down. Her eyes, sleepless and weary, blurred out of focus as she did her work in an almost hypnotic state. No decisions, no changes, just simple repetitious actions hour after hour. That factory was an inhuman valley of the shadow, where workers came to believe that the machines were running them, and not they the machines.

We humans are not intended to live a punch-press life, not at work, not at home and certainly not at church. Functioning like a machine denies the spark of God's nature deep within us. If in our personal prayers or in our corporate worship we see ourselves moving in the direction of mindless, repetitive rigidity of form, we must do everything possible to reverse the course.

Jesus' impatience over a highly rigid religious hypocrisy sizzles throughout Matthew chapter 23. Embedded in his catalogue of woes is one dealing with a liturgical fastidiousness which blindly ignores the heart of true religion. Jesus warns that the weightier matters (justice, mercy, faith) must be done, not at the expense of the lesser ones, but in vital connection with them. Jesus is not condemning a careful practice of tithing; he doesn't advise throwing away a dirty cup and plate. He urges his followers to clean and restore what is within

37

the cup, and then the outside will be clean too (Matt. 23.23,25).

The substance of religious observance has a direct relationship to its forms. Weak structures will not serve a full spirited worship. And on the other hand, overly powerful and rigid patterns can all too easily become an end in themselves, as did the religious tithing of Jesus' day.

We need forms. We need patterns that are recognisable and familiar. But those very forms can become almost tyrannous, even idolatrous. We must not allow them to take possession of our worship. Jesus said that the sabbath was made to serve, not to rule, human lives. In the same way, the ways we worship – the words, the symbols, the music and gestures we use – are not subterranean passages cut out of rock. Our ways of worship serve us in our desire to communicate with God. They are 'highways to Zion' (Ps. 84.5, RSV), ways that others have gone before, but ways that are open to fresh air and sunshine.

If it's Sunday it's got to be Church

Our worship patterns are best not modelled on coalmine tunnels. Going to church, on the other hand, should not be like entering a fairground. Too many options, too little structure and too few familiar patterns will wear people out. A kaleidoscope of variety and choice can have as deadly an effect as an over-rigid attention to 'how we've always done it'.

I'm reminded of a friendly invitation from a friend in America recently. 'Let's have a cup of something,' he said, and rattled off a bewildering array of choices. 'We have everything. These won't do you any harm: Cool Zowie, Ginger Zip, Nettle Clinch, Sipper's Choice, or Rosie's Alarm. Or if you prefer, we can do camomile, peppermint, verbena, any of those. Or how about dill, fruit, flowers, stem, root . . . ?' Realising that I was in choice-shock, he gently poured a cup of leftover coffee and pressed it into my limp hand.

How different from my friend Robert's suggestion: 'Have a cuppa?' I know just how the tea will come – dark, milky brown, slightly frothy, steaming hot – a big mug of Sainsbury's Red Label. Our drink together will last just long enough for a pleasant evening tea break.

Too much innovation in ideas or unfamiliarity in the ways of doing things in public worship can produce an effect similar to my state of 'choice overload' when offered a cup of tea.

Consider this recent experience of two of my friends. Sue and Alice were attending a stimulating seminar sponsored by a Catholic retreat centre. A get-acquainted session, an evening meal eaten in silence, followed by an introductory hour dealing with completely new concepts made the Friday a stimulating but exhausting beginning for everyone.

Early Saturday morning prayers, further development of new ideas worked out in small groups, individual sessions with the teaching sisters – all this was great for Sue. She loved meeting people, hearing new ideas, and trying out new ways of approaching questions.

But Alice was not faring so well. Although happy at first to be anonymous in the group, she soon found herself continually pushed into thinking and expressing herself in unfamiliar vocabulary or thrust into long silences which she felt unable to use in a good way.

The conference was to end with the celebration of mass. Alice was feeling the cumulative effect of too much stimulation – new books, new people, new ideas, and now it was to come to a head in a service of worship that she didn't feel at ease in. The responses were unfamiliar, the music strange. As the congregation was taking communion, someone led the chorus 'He is Lord'. Alice began to cry. Sue solicitously smiled at her, trying to understand what had touched her. Through her tears Alice whispered, 'I'm fine. I'm just happy they are singing a song I know.'

My family knows this feeling quite well. Sometimes they get 'recipe shock' after a succession of days in which I have tried one new dish after another. 'Enough of the anchovies! No more pears baked with chocolate! Just give us cheese toast and raw apples.'

Churches, too, get fed up with liturgical anchovies and strange delicacies served in rapid succession. For a while I attended a church where the weekly order of service sheet was as necessary for members as a road map for a motorist in a strange country. One never knew if a choral reading from the gallery or a procession carrying the offering forward would be the innovation of the day. The congregation was carried along by an ideology: the widest possible participation by members coupled with a steady stream of novelty creates the best worship. In those services I used to pinch myself to remember where I was. My watch told me it was Sunday, so it had to be church.

What's the Matter?

Unease and dissatisfaction with worship is affected by these two aspects: what we do and how we do it. People get tired of too much sameness or too much change. We respond partly because of the kind of personalities we are, and partly out of our past experiences.

Church committees sometimes try to understand the unease by passing around questionnaires to find out what is going on. This may prove useful. They may compile a summary of opinions. They may gain a fair knowledge of members' prejudices and ignorance. And they may put a finger on the pulse of the members' expectations and deepest wishes.

But we often find it difficult to understand what is the matter. We know without doubt when the spirit of the worship is right – there is a sense of joy and peace, a heightening sensitivity of our consciences that is a hallmark of a true meeting of God with his people. But if the spirit isn't right in our worship, we often shrug it off. 'It must have been the mood I was in.' 'Well you can't win them all.'

Answering questions about details of the worship service on a market research-style form is unlikely to get to the heart of the problem. Short responses to specific activities in a service cannot reveal enough to understand each person's feelings, let alone to make improvements in corporate worship patterns. People's background experiences, their personalities and their piety are too varied and subtle to fit into blunt answers on a photocopied questionnaire.

In some ways filling out such questionnaires is like asking conference attenders to tell in a few words what it was like coming to the conference. Some will say it was a short and easy trip (they drove a half-hour on the motorway). Others will say it was exhausting in the extreme (they rose at five a.m. had two changes on the trains, and ended with a ten minute walk up the hill carrying all their luggage). Unless we know people's journey to the place of common meeting, we can't fully understand their response to the present moment.

So it is with questionnaires about worship. They can provide a wonderful chance to deposit feelings about our past experiences in other places. But we're not writing enough of our own biographies for it to come clear. Our brief comments may turn out sounding like personal criticisms and unpleasant, uncharitable prejudice.

I know one congregation that seemed almost addicted to questionnaires. After a few years of it, their minister resigned. Amassed pages of surveys brought the message clearly to him: 'They aren't looking for leadership from me. They just want to stir the pot of their own opinions.'

If things aren't going right in our worship, we can often find the roots of the solution in the insight that Jesus gave us. True worship is 'in spirit and in truth'

(John 4.24). No amount of tinkering with forms or adjusting of sermon topics will reach the malaise of spirits out of tune with each other and with God. God is spirit; God looks on the heart; God desires truth in relationships as well as in ideas.

If God only wanted our individual worship, done in private times and places, the question of the quality of relationships in the church would have no relevance. We could worship as millions of peoples of other religions do. They go when it is convenient to perform certain ceremonies, say certain words, and give certain gifts. No sense of being a people enters into it; there is no awareness of being a family of faith.

But it isn't like that for Christians. The whole Bible is full of references to corporate life, to corporate justice, to corporate worship. We are not alone in our actions, our decisions, our pains, or our prayers. We belong to each other.

Sometimes our church reminds me of a marching band going to a festive parade. There we all are. Unfortunately, some boots are unpolished, some uniforms are without buttons, and some instruments are forgotten, left at home. We can't get out needle and thread on the spot; we can't replace a missing clarinet with an old tuba. The parade will have come and gone and the moment will have escaped for ever. So it is, if we come to worship with pent-up frustrations, bad relationships, genuine intellectual doubts, or physical agonies that are hindering our ability to enter into the corporate worship.

The church in its daily life must seek out and address the hurting points of its members. We need to find time to listen to each other and to do what Jesus did: 'Jesus wept'. We need to follow Jesus – to listen, to care, and to enter into the pain or happiness of our friends, and to pray for each other. If we do this genuinely, week by week, we can all come together for a worship service that will be marked by an almost perceptible empathy and unity. We will be genuinely aware of our solidarity in coming as needy followers of our Lord. We will be ready to make an outpouring of thankfulness for his care, no matter what our day-by-day difficulties may be. We may look a tattered band, but we will be playing in tune.

Many factors affect the 'success' of our worship. Friction among members will surface in the worship. If people are frenetic or over-busy, weary or dispirited, the worship will reflect it very quickly. The physical set-up of the furniture, the acoustics, the style of worship leading – all these play important roles in that intangible but essential quality which we refer to as the 'spirit' of worship.

But are there other factors as well? Are there specific ways to measure what has happened in a worship service which was spiritual, joyful, inspiring, peaceful, unifying and reverent? Are there some methods or techniques in planning worship that will improve the likelihood of 'success'?

Perhaps there is a parallel for us in the way a banquet is arranged. Great care is taken in laying the table, in ventilation, in proper lighting, in comfortable seating, in good food pleasantly served. None of the details of the physical setting ensures success, but each detail well prepared contributes to the possibility of a happy event. The substance of the event lies mainly in the human interaction, the social interchange. Just as there are guidelines for banquet arrangers, there can be guidelines for worship planners.

B. Form and Freedom

Liturgical Traditions

Questions of guidelines for structure go back a long way. The great liturgical traditions – Orthodox, Roman Catholic, Anglican, Lutheran – draw on just such guidelines developed many centuries ago in the early times before any of the divisions had taken place. Not arbitrary, these guidelines for worship were based on the experience of many churches in many countries. The design of the elements of worship suited the needs of the worshippers just as surely as well-designed clothing suits the needs of a desert nomad or a mountain explorer. The liturgical churches have tools and materials, venerable ones indeed, to help them arrange for worship each day, each week, each year.

An experience at an interchurch conference illustrates the way in which simple liturgical patterns can ease and serve people in a very simple way.

'Let's have a communion to close the conference this afternoon!' What a good idea, we all agreed. It had been an unusually good day, full of strong disagreements, hearty laughs, vulnerable disclosures of our places of weakness. For an interchurch group we had found a rare sense of unity in the Lord.

I slid down in my chair, hoping no one would ask me to participate in planning the service. But I needn't have worried. This planning posed no difficulty at all for Peter and Graham. They reached for their service books, inserted two readings at appropriate places, and simply decided who should lead which parts. The non-conformists were off to purchase bread and wine at the local shop. Singing a round of 'We want to bless you, we want to praise you', we were launched into a communion service memorable, even all these years later, for its sense of unity, its balance and its beauty.

Free Church Traditions

Non-liturgical Christian traditions also have guidelines, ways of doing things that have shaped their worship in distinctive ways. Some of these were formed out of positive convictions. Others were incorporated because of negative reactions, a desire not to be like certain other Christians in their ways of worship. Here are several examples that illustrate a few of the principles that underlie the shape of Free Church worship.

Soon after our arrival in England, my husband, Alan, was invited to preach one Sunday evening at a neighbouring Baptist church, which he had never visited. As he put on his tie and jacket he remarked on his unease at having to prepare a sermon for people he didn't know at all. Imagine his surprise – ignorant immigrant as he then was – upon arriving at the church to find that he was to lead the service as well as preach. Not only that. He read the Scripture, announced the hymns, prayed over the offering, and pronounced the benediction. This was called 'taking the service'. A certain simple sequence of hymns, readings, offering, and sermon was taken for granted. But beyond that the whole service rested on the one man up in the pulpit.

Singing hymns was the 'work to rule' of the congregation, while the lilt of the church secretary's voice provided a welcome relief from that of the official who was doing everything else. This kind of worship planning may yield good fruits. Certainly there could be nothing simpler than inviting someone in from the outside and asking him to do it all.

To some of us, this may seem a parody of its type, but it's not uncommon. And it isn't right to flail it. In fact this type of service is rooted in a vital tradition in which people felt a keen need to receive expert instruction in Scripture. All other parts of the service support the most important and longest part, the sermon. Other parts of the service can be pastoral, arising from the themes of the sermon and the Scripture upon which it is based. The choice of the sermon texts is crucial of course. Very often there will be a series in which many consecutive sermons will be based upon sections or indeed entire books of the Bible. The preacher is all-important, and the congregation is cast in the role of pupils in a classroom.

Another familiar non-liturgical tradition claims to use only biblical models for its apparently unstructured worship. A minister of such a church was amazed when I asked him about worship planning. 'There is no such thing,' he said. 'I just stand up in the front and proceed as the Spirit leads.' In this church, periods of singing and prayers alternate with times for healing, teaching, and prophetic words of encouragement or warning. But these things are not planned in advance. Everything is understood to be inspired by the Holy Spirit. It is illusory, however, to think that such a service is formless. Regular attenders know quite well what is likely to happen next, even though to a visitor things may seem free-flowing.

Somewhat similar to that charismatic type were early services of my tradition, the Anabaptist Mennonites. Spontaneous singing of home-produced hymns alternated with Scripture readings, silence, and periods of fervent prayer. Several members interjected exhortations based on Scriptures. One such service in eighteenth-century Pennsylvania continued all day and all night, even though the preacher had to leave around noon. Any member could contribute as the Spirit inspired.

Non-liturgical churches have clearly seen the power of worship inspired by the Spirit and centred in Scripture. Concerns of everyday life can flow into the prayers and exhortations. People hope to experience an integration of inward and outward reality. These are positive ideals for Free Church worship. When realised, they are indeed moving.

Common Ground

Even though a prayerbook communion service may seem foreign and constricting to someone used to an apparently unstructured charismatic meeting, the two types in fact have certain ideals in common. If we examine the best in both approaches we find the bases remarkably close to each other. Christians from all backgrounds agree that they meet together to honour and praise God. And they believe that the Holy Spirit breathes life into their actions, music and words.

Public worship is the body of Christ – the living corporate church – coming together to worship God, and to join the multitudes 'standing before the throne and before the Lamb, clothed in white robes with palm branches in their hands' (Rev. 7.9). Jim Punton, teasing us low-church Mennonites, once suggested that we should provide vestments for all who come to worship. Not only the ministers, he thought, should wear dazzling white, but every worshipper should have a shining garment worthy to stand before God's throne. The Aladura Christians of West Africa do exactly that. On Sundays they wear white clothing, and they form joyous and highly noticeable processions on their way to their public services. Whether or not we go in for white robes or glorious vestments donned in the vestry, we all have the privilege of wearing the mantle of praise. What a glorious vestment it is! And it is the vestment for all of us – Baptists, House Church folk, Mennonites, Anglicans and Catholics alike.

And we all agree that the Holy Spirit is the one who makes our praises possible. The Holy Spirit is the one who infuses our song and our poetry, our set prayers or our spontaneous jubilations, with the sure sense of God's presence. In the best of every tradition, Christians attempt to bring together into the presence of God the pain of the world, the suffering of those caught in webs of violence, oppression and persecution. In formal and non-formal worship alike, Christians pray fervently that unbelievers, observing the joy and healing found there, will thus be drawn into the church family and into a living faith in Jesus.

We have much to learn from each other. No one way of doing things will satisfy all the people in any one tradition. Do some feel stifled? Do some feel they can't contribute anything in an over-objective, hyper-formalised service? Are aesthetic standards, which are meant to honour God, alienating some folk? Such people will find release, freedom and a sense of belonging to the action in some of the forms of freer expression that the non-liturgical churches use.

Do people, in another church, find their services overloaded with the personal emotion of the worship leader? Do they find the public worship to be disordered and unbalanced in such a way that one week they are over-chastised and under-taught, and the following week an interminable testimony eliminated time needed for intercessory prayers? Such a church might flourish with a spirit-led balance and increased objectivity in its content.

Proper and Ordinary — a History Lesson

'But Mummy always reads a story before my bedtime drink!' little John instructs the babysitter in the routine of the Wilson household. Children are great liturgists. They love their little ways, the well-worn paths of established custom. In the bedtime routine it is by no means always the same story to be read. But John gets great satisfaction and security from the predictable sequence of events. It's the bath, the story, the drink, the toothbrush, the leap into bed, the snuggle and the kiss. 'And be sure to leave the door open just a little crack so I can see the light in the hallway.'

We adults have our little ways, too. There are the accepted sequences of work hours and breaks at the office. A birthday signals certain essential activities – the cake, the song, the wish, the candles, the clapping and finally the gifts and cards. Business meetings have ceremonies for opening, receiving of apologies for absence, reading of the minutes, and then a prescribed order of business.

We live with forms that structure our lives. The menu card in the restaurant is a simple example of how a familiar sequence can simplify things for us. The menu reduces the number of decisions we would otherwise have to make. 'What will you have to start?' the waiter asks. There are variations that can enter into the routine of ordering the first course. We can choose mushroom soup instead of tomato, but the idea of a first-course soup remains the model. We can choose desserts from the trolley, but woe betide anyone who asks for the strawberries before the stroganoff. Ordering a meal in a continental restaurant is fun, if we know the rules. There is a genuine interweaving of the known and the new. It may not be so easy when we try to order a meal in a Malaysian or African restaurant. What comes first? How do we put this meal together? We have to call for help.

Christians have been putting together the menu card of worship for 2,000 years. Within a few generations certain patterns, certain sequences of prayers and parts of the worship came into common usage quite widely throughout the churches around the Mediterranean. We have texts, fifteen and more centuries old, that show what those set parts were.

In fourth-century Antioch and Jerusalem, Christians had a little phrase they repeated after short prayer sentences. It meant 'Lord have mercy'. That phrase, kept in its original Greek form, *Kyrie eleison*, continues to this day to be part of the opening of the Christian service of Eucharist in many countries. Another bit that was incorporated early on and came to be used widely, was the angels' song recorded in Luke's gospel: 'Glory to God in the highest'. The mysterious 'Holy, holy, holy' from Isaiah chapter 6, and John the Baptist's words: 'Behold the Lamb of God who takes away the sin of the world' (John 1.35). Between the fourth and seventh centuries were incorporated into Christian communion services.

These regularly recurring segments of Scripture (the set or *ordinary* bits) formed a familiar framework for the service around which other parts fitted in. From week to week the other parts changed and were inserted as appropriate. Other services of the church besides the Eucharist also have unchanging parts: in morning or evening prayer services, certain psalms or New Testament hymns are always used. These repeated parts are called the 'ordinary' parts.

But every service also had its variable parts. Churches developed cycles of readings for the Psalms and for Old and New Testament. These readings fitted around the 'ordinary' parts. The variable bits signal the different seasons of the year: there are lots of 'alleluias' in the Easter season. Penitential and introspective psalms are prominent in Lent. The variable parts are appropriate, *proper*, to the particular day and season. That is why they are called 'propers'.

This variation is what makes it hard for some visitors to follow the services of the liturgical churches. If the leader doesn't help by clearly noting which special psalm and which particular prayer for the day is coming next, the visitors can get in a muddle.

Ordinaries and propers are the warp and woof of Christian liturgical services. They represent something similar to the way we live in other aspects of our life. The familiar and the new; the expected and the novel; the foot we are standing on and the foot that steps ahead – these are natural to life. They provide both the stability and the dynamic quality that we need.

C. Planning a Service

Christians these days often work together in preparing special services. Sometimes they are planning one in support of an international relief project, or as part of a community-based evangelistic programme. At other times their focus is a seasonal celebration or as the climax of a retreat weekend. Christians in the non-liturgical traditions have their Sunday services to plan. All of us, at one time or another, have occasion to establish good ways of planning worship services.

Working together with people from different churches poses special questions. But we can face these more easily if we have thought through how we plan worship within our own churches. For some, who are in churches where the minister does all the preparation, this may be an irrelevant question. But even in such a situation, it is useful to observe and consider in some detail how thoughtful preparation can enrich a church's worship.

Here, for an example, is the way our church goes about planning. It is a general plan which over a period of several years has become familiar to the members of its worship-planning group. It provides a place for the aspects of worship that the members feel are essential to every service. It also embodies certain principles which may not be obvious to a visitor, but which underlie the quality of life within the membership of the church.

This set of principles and worship plan are not meant to be an ideal. They belong to a particular congregation, and they reflect the special characteristics of that group of people in their worship. But perhaps it will be useful to others to observe the way this church has thought about its principles, ethos, leadership and the incorporation of its members' gifts in worship. First, a look at the principles that undergird the worship planning:

Principles

1 Direct attention towards God, away from person leading.
2 Be flexible within the form.
3 Foster a corporate experience.
4 Bring a wide range of everyday experiences into the worship.
5 Maintain a balance between 'thoughts' and 'feelings'.

6 Foster homeliness, but not at the expense of God's 'otherness'.
7 Include a variety of types of prayers.
8 Allow an open time for members to speak freely.
9 Incorporate silent points for listening and reflection.
10 Make generous use of Scripture, in all sections of service.
11 Encourage variety in methods of teaching and preaching.
12 Plan for participation by many – in readings, prayers, music, etc.
13 Encourage creativity, providing a place for expressing members' gifts in music, poetry, visual art, dance and drama.
14 Watch language – be inclusive, clear, direct, appropriate.
15 Expect the worship to affect the everyday life of members.
16 Ensure that a significant part of the worship is accessible to all ages.
17 Expect the Holy Spirit to 'fire' the worship.

Possible Service Plan

I *First Section*
   a Gathering songs
   b Opening Scripture
   c Prayer
   d Songs or hymns
   e Theme of service
   f Scripture
   g Welcome to guests
   h Activity (story, drama, etc.)
   i Offering
   j Songs

II Second Section
   k Open time
   l Prayers (of various types)

III Third Section
   m Scripture
   n Sermon
   o Song or hymn
   p Closing
or *III Third Section (Communion)*
   m Homily
   n Exchanging the peace
   o Service of bread and wine
   p Song or hymn
   q Closing

Each of the three sections takes up about one-third of the total time of the service. The entire First Section is designed so that people of all ages can understand and take part in a meaningful way. The Second Section includes an open time and several types of prayers. The Third Section is shaped either as a communion service or as a sermon and benediction. We will look a bit more closely at some details of this plan, to illustrate how the parts are actually worked out.

In the First Section the opening music part (a) is intended to gather people together and bring their attention into focus for worship. The music sets the temper and tone of the service. Singing together brings a sense of unity.

The first spoken words are words of Scripture (b), chosen as a call to praise and unity in the presence of God. These are followed by a short prayer (c) of thanks and anticipation of the benefits and joy of worship.

Further songs and explanation of the theme of the service (d and e) bring children and adults together around a simple idea of God's relationship to us (e.g. God as our creator, God as our protector), or around a parable of Jesus or some other Bible story. A short

Bible reading (f) grounds the theme. This may be read by one of the children.

We welcome guests and then briefly describe what may happen during the worship. This can set people, particularly guests, at ease. A dramatic reading or story follows, (h), to underline the theme of the day, along with a song, dance, or artifact that makes the theme as tangible and visual as possible. This section is often extrovert in tone, and has a celebratory and relaxed atmosphere.

The First Section is intended to appeal to the children, and to the child within each adult. As much as possible, the medium for the various components is dramatic or visual. The result is not childish, and certainly not silly.

As the planning and preparation proceeds, the guideline is always to have things simple, clear, and done with the awareness that children are present. This does not mean that everything has to be totally comprehensible to a seven-year-old child. But it does mean that whatever is done is done with sensitivity to the children present. Service planning that aims 'down' at children does them a disservice. Too often, then, the result is an insult to the children and an embarrassment to the adults.

Section Two includes an open time for people to tell their concerns and experiences, and to give testimony. Prayers of various kinds follow, sometimes concluded with a sung version of the Lord's Prayer. The atmosphere of this period is usually quiet, reflective, perhaps introspective. To achieve continuity and comprehensiveness, a small group of members takes responsibility for leading this section. In this section, prayers of confession, healing, intercession for the Church and the world, and attentiveness to answered prayers all find their place. Anyone present can express concerns and feelings from daily life as explicitly and sensitively as possible.

This section, the prayers of the Church, is the workshop of the service. The Church's assignment, after all, is to pray for the world, for the neighbour, for the alien, for the enemy, for those in governing power, for other Christians, for prisoners and for themselves. This is a big responsibility, and cannot be discharged by a few hurried petitions which are sandwiched between more urgent agenda items.

Section Three may be a communion service. Alternatively, this section may centre around the sermon with its attendant Scripture reading, and appropriate hymn or song to follow. If possible, there is time for quiet after the sermon, and sometimes an opportunity for verbal response as well. The section closes with a passage of Scripture that summarises the theme of the day, and which encourages and sends the people out with a blessing, in the peace of Christ.

This description of principles and plan may sound obvious and ordinary. It should be. To the congregation that uses it, it is as familiar as an old shoe. That is what it means for them to be 'at home' with it. Visitors and members alike can feel this ease and familiarity.

Certain features are essential for the planning and preparation of a service. A fundamental point is that several people, not just one person, work on the plans together. Continuity in the planning group is important, but new members need to come into it. In this way the worship, over a period of time, will take on the thumbprint of the entire group, not just the idiosyncrasies of an individual who happens to be responsible on a particular day.

This method of worship planning, with a number of people committing their time, week after week, is costly. But how valuable their contribution is! The planners are not performers or manipulators; they are truly servants of their church.

D. Leadership Styles

Follow the leader is a favourite children's game. Everyone has a chance to play the leader and also to be a follower. Even if we don't think of ourselves as potential prime ministers we all know some situations in which we must make decisions about what is to happen next, and about what action is required to bring it about. No matter if it is trying to get two little children into the back seat of the car or dispatching drivers onto their delivery rounds, we have choices to make about leadership. We need to decide how loudly to talk, or when to use a gesture instead of words; we need to choose what is appropriate to the situation.

Worship leaders have many decisions to make. Sometimes the apparently small ones are the very ones that have the most effect. All too often the first spoken words are personal pronouns which call attention to the leader. I once heard a worship leader begin like this: 'Now I want you all to close your eyes and think about two or three things that you did this week that make you feel ashamed. In a few minutes we are going to make our confession to God, and we need to be specific about our shortcomings. It's no good asking God just to forgive us in general.' People don't like being harangued in church, and the worshippers will turn off the worship leader who scolds them. The first decision in preparation is to choose words which point to God and to deliver them in a suitable tone of voice.

This might be a slightly better opening line than the one above, but it is in the same 'teachy' vein. 'The psalmist tells us that God is to be everywhere worshipped and adored. So now let's worship God by opening our green books to number twenty-three. I'm going to ask the musicians to play it through once before we sing so that each one of us can read the lines of the first verse as they go along. We can apply to ourselves this wonderful call to worship. After that we will sing all four verses of the song. All right, musicians, you can begin.'

That sounded like instructions in a classroom. There is a better way to employ the idea of God being everywhere worshipped and adored than by calling for a song by the colour of the book and the number. Why not simply allow a Bible text that is similar, or a line from the hymn itself (but not an entire stanza) to function as the call to worship? Is it any wonder we feel ill at ease, manipulated by well-intentioned but wordy and clumsy leadership?

Why do we worshippers so easily fall into this mode of spectators, or of participants in a keep-fit class? Perhaps it is that we have all spent many years under the authority and verbal style of teachers and headmasters; their often hectoring habits of speech are an obvious influence. Similarly, the MCs and toastmasters of formal dinners or television entertainments serve as models; from them we learn to entertain and cajole. The pace and flow of the talk-show host cannot but dazzle us and make us, even unconsciously, strive for a similar slickness and quick timing.

Sometimes, even if unintentionally, the leader draws the worshippers' main attention to himself; and thus he defeats his purpose for being there at all. The first word that comes out of the leader's mouth is often the most revealing one. If a pronoun, first person singular, comes first, it may well be followed by a parallel 'my' 'we', 'mine' or 'me', as for example: 'I am happy to see so many of you here this morning. As I said to my wife on our way to church . . .' This kind of opening is suitable for an after-dinner speech at a family reunion. It is informal, personal, relaxed. Though none of these qualities in itself is inimical to worship leading, it is the style of the delivery which is inappropriate.

Sometimes the leader will scold people for being late, tell a joke, or ostentatiously move folk about in the room. If people are late, looking glum, or sitting in the wrong place, there may be good reason to rectify the underlying causes. But surely the worship leader would do better to make a mental note of the conditions and then proceed with poise into the task at hand.

Consciously or unconsciously, everyone knows the unease caused by inept, manipulative, intrusive, scolding or self-promoting worship leaders. No worship leader ever means to be like that. It takes more than good intentions, however, to be an effective servant as the leader of a congregation's worship.

As a worship leader, I am serving the people as one who helps to prepare the context in which they can meet God. Any temptation to teach or scold is a trapdoor to failure and offence. I have avoided falling through the floor if I am like the minister in the wedding photo, holding the joined hands of the couple aloft. As worship leader I am to be a go-between in what may well become the most important encounter of the week.

Serving as a go-between can be a good mental image for all worship leaders, whether in liturgical or Free Church worship. To put it in a slightly different way, we could consider the example of a famous orchestral conductor whom I recently saw at a concert.

If I stopped to think about it, I realised, of course, that the maestro was fully in charge. He was directing the speed and the varying loudness. He was in command of all the details of a complex musical piece. But, so unobtrusively did he exercise his conducting skill, my eyes were not drawn to him. The music flowed through him. It was not obstructed or distorted by a manipulative style. My ears and my heart responded to the music; they were never impeded by the individual quirks of the conductor's personality. To use an electrical analogy, he was a conductor, not a resistor!

E. Songs Ancient and Brand New

When it is Good, it is Very, Very Good . . .
Music is powerful. It can be like electricity, destructive and blinding when improperly channelled. But at its best, music is illuminating and energising. It can be a source of unity, a vehicle for devotion in worship. It can be a medium for creativity and joy. Music can enable people to participate in public worship in ways otherwise unavailable to them. It can be for everyone, not just for the special few.

For centuries, music sung by a whole congregation in conjunction with poetry or biblical texts has been an indispensable part of Christian worship. Worship is significantly hampered for many Christians if there is no chance to sing a psalm, a hymn or a song. Why do we so much enjoy singing in church? What is congregational music's unique contribution to our worship?

For one thing, singing is something we do together. We agree on the tune, the pitch and the speed. Everyone, from the youngest to the oldest, can take part. Of all the things we do in worship, singing together is the most genuinely corporate. How that corporateness is understood may vary, however. Dietrich Bonhoeffer delighted in the unity expressed through unison singing (everyone sings the melody).[10] But Mennonites explain that their four-part, unaccompanied singing symbolises the diversity of gifts within the body of Christ.

Singing together is enjoyable. And best of all, when we all sing together, no critic stands there to make judgments. Church music is not a performance; it is a gift. And it is a two-way gift. Music is God's gift to us, and it can be our gift to him too. God receives our music, not as entries in a competition, but as the offerings of thoughtfulness and love of people whose lives mean everything to him.

How well I remember, when I was a child, my father

bargaining with me after mealtimes. He would wash up the dishes – if I would play the piano for him. Knowing his pleasure in my music helped me to play my best. When God listens to our congregational singing he listens not as a critic, but as a loving parent. Knowing this, we are inspired to do our best and to sing our hearts out.

And when we sing wholeheartedly to God, he responds. He enlivens the music with his Spirit. My friend Fred recently illustrated this in a sermon. He had attended a service which moved him deeply. Since his wife was away on that day, he borrowed a tape recording of the service. 'The sermon was good, and the music was especially wonderful that day!' he told her. Listening together at home, they agreed that the sermon was indeed good. But what had happened to the singing? Individual voices stuck out: all sorts of things were wrong. It just didn't sound as good as he had remembered it. Fred is convinced that the Spirit, who was present in the service, made the worship come alive in a way the tape couldn't begin to recapture.

Conflict over Music.

Music, like prayer and food, belongs to everybody. Music carries memories and evokes devotion. It stimulates peacefulness or anger, joy or horror. Virtually everybody has opinions about music, a favourite song, and probably a pet hate as well. Terrible disputes in families and neighbourhoods erupt because of intolerance of others' musical tastes. It's not surprising, then, that music can cause havoc in our churches as well. When church music goes badly, intense feelings boil over.

I recently heard extreme frustration over music when visiting a friend's church. 'I hate music in church!' said Jim. 'It's the most divisive thing in our congregation!'

I couldn't believe my ears. Surely Jim was exaggerating. Music? Divisive? I never think of music that way.

Doesn't music bring people together, singing in the choir, choosing favourites around the piano . . .

'. . . and the rest of the congregation just sit there,' he continued, 'with their mouths clamped tight shut. The young people spend so much time playing and singing that several of them even want to pursue music professionally. None of them want to become Bible teachers or pastors. Now if it were up to me, I'd dismiss the musicians and the whole choir today. I'd forbid singing. We'd just have readings and sermons and discussions. Or even better, just plain silence.'

Jim's tirade continued with drastic solutions to the 'music problem'. I suggested that he probably would have been happier as a Christian in the second century, when only unaccompanied, unison singing was allowed in the churches.[11] He was not amused.

. . . When it is Bad, it is Horrible!

Music can be good or it can be horrible. Why does it often fail to serve us in our worship?

One reason is that sometimes the music *is* horrible. Without thought and adequate preparation, music has little chance to serve as a worthy gift. Often hymns or songs are chosen solely for the text, with no regard for their musical settings. For example, after singing three successive songs, a congregation may not know why they seemed dull. Musicians could quickly point out that all the songs were in the same key, or in too similar metric and rhythmic patterns. Careful attention to sequence of musical settings enlivens congregational music immeasurably. Speed, loudness, instrumentation, pitch range of the melody, quickness of harmonic changes – these are just a few important musical factors which worship leaders should consider.

An extreme example of hymns chosen purely because of the texts was a service in which I served as piano accompanist. In the course of the morning the minister announced three hymns, all set to the same tune. Reaction ranged from disbelief to giggling and annoyance.

Conversely, the music can rule the choices. In this case we have an indigestible succession of old favourites just because they are easy to sing. Or the choices may be quirky, having nothing to do with the theme of the service. On Sunday evenings when Chris, a song leader in my childhood church stood up, we always knew we would sing 'Now the day is over.' It has an irresistible bass part which Chris himself liked to sing, much more interesting than the soprano's line. So we all learned bass. I wonder how many congregations know the words of that hymn to the bass melody?

Many church musicians have written and taught, demonstrated and rehearsed what must go into good church music. Careless or shoddy music is just as bad as a poorly prepared sermon. Music and words alike can be an embarrassment to the congregation and an affront to the God whom we worship. Let us learn to take care in our choice and preparation of music. Music is a gift.

A Mix of Old and New

Further reasons that music fails to serve us have to do with our variety of personalities and our experience. Some people thoroughly enjoy learning new songs. Others, confronted by 'yet another new one', go on strike! Our responses to tradition and to change are so different. Some of us would rather everything stayed the same while the rest would prefer to try something new.

Reasons for our attitudes to old songs are often hidden. Some members of the church hate hymns because of childhood associations with school assembly. Old hymns transport others back to another world, which now seems to have been more placid and manageable. And some new songs get worn out very quickly. They're like paper towels – they're suitable for one job, but they disintegrate with use!

What older music should we continue to use? We must discriminate carefully. Judging a text requires more than pleasant familiarity or an association with a favoured elderly relative. Does the text convey something significant with vividness and truth? Sentiment isn't enough.

Songs written to confront or comfort people in situations utterly unlike our own may not be useful to Christians today. On the other hand, hymns and songs from other places and times can deepen our empathy with the breadth of human experience. It is the same with singing the Psalms. They reflect universal human experiences and a universal search for God.

A healthy repertoire of music includes hymns from the ancient church, songs from Christians of other countries, hymns from virtually every past century, and a continuous stream of new songs. Singing now with Christians around the world and through ages past is one way of realising in advance the joy of the inter-tribal hymn-sing around the throne of the Lamb!

When church members travel abroad, they can actively search out souvenir songs from churches they have visited. A cassette tape of South American Christians singing their own music enlivened a recent slide show in our church. We could learn their songs and use them to enrich our worship.

One of our members spent a summer in South Africa as a volunteer worker. While there, he wrote several songs which expressed his response to what he saw and learned. When he came home and taught the songs to the church, we connected ourselves strongly both to him, our brother, and to his experiences. Writing new songs like this and singing them together did more than simply broaden our musical capacities. We encouraged a creative gift in our own church, and at the same time we expressed solidarity with Christians in other countries.

A few members can research the historic hymns of a church's tradition, and restore a tangible link to its own past. The hymns we sing are a vital means of passing on the story of our church.

If these examples don't have parallels in your church's musical life, don't worry. You can work towards such a goal over a number of years, and the going is good on the way. But if our musical diet isn't carefully balanced with new and old music, we will hear dissatisfaction. The challenge is to introduce novelty in the right amount for your congregation.

New Music

But how much new music is 'the right amount'? We always measure the novel by the familiar. It's striking that churches which already know a great deal of music often seem able to learn new music more easily. Taking stock of the modern songs a church knows, apart from the traditional hymns, can be surprising. Many churches have a repertoire of several hundred such 'new' songs. It is a rich church that can draw out of its music storehouse the new as well as the old.

A new song or hymn can quickly become a part of a church's tradition as we make associations with it. In our church the hymn, 'O Young and Fearless Prophet', reminds us of Saadi, for whom this text was vital in his search for Jesus. And we smile as we sing it, remembering our hapless pianist who tried to play it without its flats.

One summer, when we had a series of sermons based on Hosea, a couple of members collaborated in writing a song which captured the message of the book: 'We will return to you, for you are our God. We maintain love and justice, and wait in faith for you.' Now, as we sing this refrain of the song, we remember not only Hosea's message, but our pleasure in writing and learning it.

A hymn can convey a church's history and sense of identity. 'Great is thy faithfulness' has almost become our church's theme-hymn. We have so often sung it at important events – at weddings, when we have moved to a new meeting place, or when we have said goodbye to people moving away.

Whenever there is life in a church, creativity will flourish. And that means among other things, new songs. Many a song has been written down at one rush, or has come springing out of a dream, fully complete. Sometimes the careful, even corporate, crafting of a song marks the spirit's work in a congregation. Some churches might want to follow the lead of St Michael-le-Belfry (York) and establish a song-writers' group. In it ideas for songs, the craft of composition and refining of detail enable musical creativity in the Church. Where the Spirit of the Lord is at work, there will be musical and poetic inspiration.

We should expect the Spirit to give us new visions that will take us beyond the confines of the theology of traditional hymnody. And what big gaps there are to fill! In traditional hymns, for example, there is an overwhelming emphasis on the grace of God who forgives us. But there is an astounding lack of emphasis on the forgiveness which we offer to each other. These themes are both important in Jesus' teaching. Who would say the story of the 'forgiving Father' is more profound than the story of the 'ungrateful servant' who, after having being forgiven his debt, throttled the colleague who owed him a pittance?

Similarly, in traditional songs and hymns, there is a potent emphasis on the justice of God and the peace which he puts into our hearts. But where are the songs which call upon God to bring justice to the oppressed in our land? And which hymns equip us to be justice-makers and peacemakers in God's image? Our songs reflect our theology. If our heads are in the clouds, that's where we can expect our music to be. The Bible – the whole Bible – should be our mine of themes for our new songs of worship.

Every church probably has its composers and poets.

They need a push, or at least an invitation, to get them going. Why not commission some new songs for next Christmas or One World Week? Why not invite the children to compose? If the music in your church is dull or horrible, pray for the Spirit to give a gift of creativity. We humans are made in the image of God, and creativity is one facet of this image. So let's expect new songs, compose them, sing them, appreciate them, evaluate them and share them with others.

It's no pleasure to visit one church and then another, and hear exactly the same songs in each place. That's like finding the same three plaster ducks flying on everyone's living-room walls. Churches have great variety in their architecture and visual decoration. They have unique verbal styles in their preachers and worship leaders. This is good. Churches should have distinctive musical personalities, too.

Throwaway Music

Many songs, meaningful and good as they might be, have their useful moment, and then they disappear. We shouldn't regret this. For centuries, short-lived, throw-away music has been a reality for composers and performers. Think of all the musicians in the minstrels' galleries of great halls and palaces. Remember the street musicians, or the virtuoso improvisers in a hundred organ lofts. Especially before recording technologies were developed, music was for the moment of its performance alone. Music is one of the most transitory of the arts: all musicians have to work within this quality. How many marvellous performances are prepared, played, heard, and then vanish into the ether? This doesn't mean that the performances were unworthy or without value. It just means that they had their moment, full of meaning because of the experience of inspiration or enjoyment or worship in which they were used. Their moment – that was enough.

66

Similarly, some newly composed church songs, like songs composed in the secular world, will not last. Still, in every era the Church needs new music. We need music in the idiom of our own time. It might not turn out to be that rare thing – a 'classic' that we return to year in and year out. But who can tell?

One of the best ways towards a vital musical life in a church is for members to appreciate and to encourage musical creativity. If we pray for inspiration for our poets and our musicians, God will honour our prayers. The Holy Spirit has a huge store of song ideas for the churches. Some songs will be easy and enjoyable choruses. Others will be sobering and will challenge our thoughts and lifestyle. Let's pray, encourage the gifts and expect our public worship to burst out with 'new songs to the Lord.'

Musical Prayer

Is some music intrinsically more 'Spirit-filled', or more prayerful than other music? Possibly. But when we describe a piece of music in this way we may, above all, reflect our own experience in using that music in worship. Other people will have similar associations, but with different types of songs. So we must not be too dogmatic in our judgments. Yet, for all of us, there has been something in the marriage of text and tune which has enabled us to communicate with God. What is this quality in the songs we sing?

It is intangible, and hard to describe. Music is available for our use, to be our servant, in our communication with God. A certain song or hymn can serve us well in one circumstance, but in the wrong setting, it can create barriers in worship. Our Spirit-led capacity to discriminate, along with our attitudes in singing, leading, or playing, will make all the difference. As we grow in our ability to pray, we will find that a greater variety of types of music can help us.

Sometimes we want music to express our quiet, inner

joy. At other times music helps us to expand a bigger, corporate thanksgiving, connecting with 'all the saints'. We may need music for processions or dances. What hymn or song shall we choose? An index of all the music known in the Church, by categories (quiet praise, loud praise, procession, meditative prayer, short response, etc.) is useful to both worship leaders and musicians.

Meditative Singing
Music can aid meditative prayer. Obviously, traditional hymns of four or five verses are not suited for this purpose. The music's harmonic change is often too quick. And the ideas go by much too fast. No, hymns based on complex or subtle poetry have another, (though equally important) place. But songs with a simple or at least a single idea are of great help in meditative periods of worship.

Trained musicians often find this difficult to believe. I remember well my earlier annoyance at songs whose text was repetitive and whose music seemed trite. Singing 'Jesus, Jesus' over and over sounded ridiculous! But gradually I discovered that repeating these words in a simple musical setting, indeed focused my attention on Jesus. To pray in a more profound way, I needed to repent of my musically trained pride; I needed to choose simplicity. Sometimes, I discovered, an artless song of prayer – in contrast to a complex anthem or hymn – can prove that 'less is more'. Learning about the 'Jesus Prayer' of Orthodox spirituality reinforced this discovery. And still more recently, I have found the music of the Taizé Community – so widely used among the youth of Europe – to be a vehicle of extended, corporate, musical prayer.[12] It has moved me.

In all of this, the goal of church musicians is a simple one: to serve the people. Musicians can play in such a way that people feel so much at ease with their music that they can concentrate their attention upon God.

They will not marvel at the elaborateness of an arrangement, the dexterity of the players, or the inventiveness of musical improvisations. The aim, for musicians and congregation alike, is to allow the medium of music to enhance their experience of God in worship.

F.   Family Worship

Children's church? When I was a child no one had heard of such a thing. No one took us out halfway through the long service, to ply us with apple juice and snacks, or to edify us with moral tales which we could comprehend. Not one attempt was made to acknowledge that children were present in church services. This was in keeping with the general way in which parents brought up children. Parents were not self conscious about their parental roles. Church was church, and the children just went along and sat quietly while it all happened around them.

Of course, this could be a spur to ingenuity. Some of my friends smuggled photos of their friends into the services. They also winked and wrote notes to one another. I can remember passing the time by counting the moles on my arms. Did I have more on my right arm than on my left? Then I checked my pulse against the big clock on the side wall. I wasn't much good at maths, but I always tried to add up the hymn numbers on the board. Then I'd estimate how many people, if they all pushed together, could actually be crammed into the rows ahead. Folding little dolls in a swinging cradle made from my pink and orange handkerchief always took a while. Then with a big sigh I gazed at the preacher, hoping against hope that he would close his big Bible and announce the closing hymn.

But we're in a new era. Parents think carefully about how they raise their children. Toy shops have become 'early learning centres'. Specialist teachers prepare materials carefully graded for the different stages of perception as the children mature. It is not enough to say, 'Well, I had to sit through church, so my kids are going to have to do the same.' Today we realise that children are people. We are aware of the opportunity to use our time together so that every person present, whatever age or condition, can be drawn into the activity of worship.

Every Person Drawn in, Regardless of Age
Churches are finding creative ways to do this. Churches that have large memberships, with dozens of children at various stages, and specialised task-oriented teams of workers (banner group, music group, dance group) can mount frequent and effective 'family worship' services.

One such large church has family worship every Sunday morning. It is a service to which the children go with eagerness, knowing that they will be able to sing the songs, listen to the stories, play in the little orchestra, do a dance, choose a birthday song, and, with the rest of the family, say the prayers. It is wonderful to see the joy and the expectation on the faces of the children of this church. Their Sunday school has moved to Friday evenings. At that time the children are prepared for the theme of the Sunday service. When they come to worship, they know that the service will genuinely be for them.

Family worship like that, though wonderfully inclusive for children and parents, can alienate others, particularly people who are not in young, nuclear families. Sometimes a regular, informal, service will cause a virtual division of the congregation into two groups: those who have direct links with children and those without children. In the church described above, the Sunday evening service is a relaxed, two-hour period which incorporates a time of prayer, readings, testimonies, and a teaching – all things that are specifically geared to the needs of adults. All those children from the morning service are at home in bed. This service is not a family service.

Providing separately for family worship and adult worship, thus has drawbacks as well as benefits. Worship should be a unifying point for the church, and not the reverse.

Some churches find the regular preparation for special all-age services to be too time-consuming or the services themselves too 'folksy', so they arrange family services less frequently. Yet other churches set aside a brief period in the regular worship hour as the children's time. Here they often ask the children to come forward in front of the whole congregation where they have a 'spot' devised especially for them.

This arrangement poses special difficulties. The mixing of an intimate setting (a story teller with ten children gathered around her) with a whole crowd of people listening is daunting. The storyteller may play to the galleries or may have to speak too loudly. The children may be offended by adult laughter at their innocent responses. Unfortunately, the message implicit in this way of doing things is that the rest of the service is *not* for the children, so their attention can be diverted with games or books. Anything to keep them quiet!

A more drastic approach is the one described by Julia and Robert Banks in the Home Church movement in Australia.[13] Their principle is that a church should remain small and home-sized. Everyone, whether child or adult, is an equal member of a home church. Children and adults are integrated in all activities. Worship reflects the pilgrimage of faith – the children hear the Bible stories, sing the songs, remain present during fervent prayer, feel the tug and pull of discussion and share the quietness and the laughter of what these people call 'family' worship. Eating a meal together which is eucharistic and joyful, and which

71

genuinely expresses the sharing of life, playing games together after lunch – these are expressions of a family at worship, in the setting of a home.

After all, the home is itself a potent symbol. Home is where people live. It's a place of safety and provision, of work and rest. Home is a place where relationships can flourish. Worshipping in the home, Christians can naturally bring their everyday concerns into the presence of God, the One who wants to comfort and inspire his people.

The Child in Ourselves

But let's broaden the picture. We need to go beyond just arranging something for the kids, and assuming that all the other things we do are all right for the adults. We have all been children ourselves. We would like to think we've grown out of some aspects of the naiveté of childhood. But there are big parts of ourselves which can and should remain childlike. As Jesus said, we can only enter the kingdom when we become as little children (Matt. 18.3).

It's all right to let the child in us come to worship. It's also all right to plan public worship with a child's perceptions in mind – the simplicity, the imagination, the preference for visual and practical illustration. All of us had these qualities at an earlier stage of life. And even though school and our upbringing have induced us to suppress them in favour of verbal and logical ways of looking at the world, we can find wholeness as we, by God's grace, recover some of what we have lost.

'He did not say anything to them without using a parable' (Mark 4.34). Did Jesus insult his hearers by using stories, and exclusively stories, when he taught? No. Jesus was the master of a form of communication which has burned his ideas into the memories of his followers over twenty centuries, and across many cultures. Sometimes his stories were original. Sometimes he revised parables from other sources. And sometimes Jesus used current incidents or acted out his own parables. We would do well to re-tell these stories, to immerse ourselves in the forms and images which Jesus chose to convey the reality of God and the meaning of his kingdom. Jesus' stories should be a central and integral part of our public worship, accessible to adults and children alike. The meaning of the stories grows and deepens as we experience more of life, but the stories are just as true for the young as for the old.

'A Little Child Will Lead Them'

People often observe that the adults enjoy the 'children's time' as much as the children. In our church we have a musical setting for the Lord's Prayer which includes actions that enhance the meaning of the text. These motions were first introduced to make adult worship more accessible to children. In the end, this had made the Lord's Prayer more full of meaning to both adults and children.

In a natural setting, children do not mask their reactions to what is going on. They show delight or anger more spontaneously than we adults. It has been wonderful to see the members of our church grow in their ability to express emotional response to what is said, prayed for and read. Tears, groans, laughter, even cheers are not uncommon. And this is, to a significant extent, because we are trying to 'change and become as little children' (Matt. 18.3) in our worship.

The challenge to us all is this: to broaden and humanise the breadth of emotional expression in worship. We go to church as whole persons, and we take all that we are along with us. Consciously or subconsciously, we take our own personal worlds into our corporate worship. It's so much richer if we consciously bring our concerns and our emotions into the light of day! In this, as in so much else, children can show us the way.

For Thought and Action

Can you differentiate between a familiar worship pattern and one which exerts tyranny?

At what point might creative change become destructive and alienating? How do you determine the right amount of novelty in worship forms?

Does your church allow gifts within the church to help determine the forms of worship?

List qualities and principles that underlie your corporate worship. Is there a balance between regular and novel elements in each service? What contributes to the typical atmosphere of worship?

If wide participation is valued, how can your church train and encourage the many gifts that will enable it?

Is it possible to establish a forum for expressing reactions and listening to feedback from your public worship?

Do you encourage a variety of music in worship?

Try forming a musical band of instrumentalists and singers which crosses the age span, leads music of many types.

Commission poems and music for specific events and seasons of the year.

Search through collections of old hymns and songs. Get to know your own historic tradition.

Write new words to familiar and folk tunes.

Ask the children to compose songs.

Bring songs back as souvenirs from travels abroad.

Dramatise Bible stories in worship.

Encourage visual and symbolic means to express truth.

Work with simplicity and imagination rather than with 'professional' and complex methods.

Tell stories – from your own past, from your neighbourhoods. Use story games, mimes, charades, modern adaptations of Bible stories, stories from churches in other countries.

Incorporate silence with the children. Find ways to express sadness and sympathy in all-age worship periods.

3. Bible Words in Worship

Planning for corporate worship is like building a campfire. Just as we gather the kindling for a fire, we need to choose carefully our Bible portions for worship. As we plan the prayers, the hymns and the songs, we need to let in plenty of space and air. Too many words without silences between will make our worship fire smoke and choke.

The sticks and logs for the worship fire are the Bible verses. Just as the kindling and the wood can't make themselves into a fire, so the words of the Bible have no power in themselves. They are not alive. Only as the breath of God sets the fire alight can the words of his *Word* communicate. Only then can they burn and purge, warm and lighten our lives.

Let's build a fire! This book is about how we can build corporate worship fires. This section is about how the Bible can work in our worship. It is about how to prepare readings, prayers, and meditations which may enable the spirit of God to use this priceless fuel to bring light, warmth, and energy into our worship.

A. How Christians Have Done It

The Bible in the Liturgical Churches
Bible words have always been stepping stones for worshippers. Hundreds of years before Christ, the Hebrews had their treasury of psalms. Because the earliest Christians were Jews, they brought their precious psalms with them. Descriptions of first-century Christian worship bear this out.

Psalms new and ancient, 'memoirs of the apostles' (the gospels) and 'writings of the prophets' (Old Testament prophets) form important segments of the worship of the Church in Rome as described in the mid-second century by Justin Martyr.[14] Basil of Caesarea, a fourth-century bishop, was a profound teacher of the Bible. He reshaped the worship of his churches, enriching it with infusions of Scripture. Bible texts, deep sources for spirituality, were also safeguards for right doctrine.[15] People needed to immerse themselves in pure Bible, and to express their worship in the richest words possible – the words of Scripture.

For centuries Christians have kept this rich heritage of worship brim full of Bible words. In the liturgical traditions, psalms, readings from both testaments, biblical canticles and benedictions have been the predominant medium of worship. Non-biblical words – prayers and sermons – have been relatively less important. One of the great strengths of these ancient services is that their beauty and power – the beauty and power of the Bible – can come through almost regardless of the abilities of the people in charge of the services.

In earliest times, leaders of Christian worship were instructed to pray 'as far as they are able', or 'as long as time permits', thus combining form with freedom.[16] But eventually the churches' leaders decided that it was better to prescribe the prayers and limit the extempore words. Bible words were dependable, potent, inspiring – and universal.

Bible in the Free Churches
The churches born in the sixteenth-century Reformation have always insisted that their worship is rooted in Scripture. The Bible is central to the nurture of the Christian life. Cottage Bible study groups, Sunday schools, Bible memory camps, Bible knowledge contests, 'sword drills' – all these have had their place in

77

different generations' attempts to be sure that all the people knew their Bibles well.

Enormous sermons devoted to Bible exposition demonstrated the centrality of Scripture. In post-Reformation England some pulpits were fitted with a big hour glass in full view of the congregation. This was not to warn the preacher when he had gone on too long, but to assure the people that they had got their money's worth – a full hour! The Bible was central, and expounding it was the most important feature of public worship.

The Bible was at the heart of individual piety, too. Over many years people have profited from the use of carefully laid out Bible reading schemes for their private devotions. The Scripture Union and the Bible Society, for example, have published popular materials for this purpose. Besides individual guides there are lesson plans and teaching schemes prepared for Bible study groups and adult Sunday school classes.

Free Church Christians have always considered the Bible as a primary focus in their worship. Their emphasis has been on explanations of the texts, intellectual understanding and application to everyday piety. They want their Bibles explained to them in terms that are simple, reasonable, and practical.

B. Using the Bible — Strengths and Weaknesses

Strengths and weaknesses appear in the ways that all Christian traditions use Scripture. The following examples and stories will illustrate this, and may point some ways forward for all of us.

Patterns of Scripture Readings
Regular and systematic reading of the Psalms is one of the most ancient aspects of our worship. It is rooted deeply in Jewish worship. Early Christians, being devout Jews, adopted this practice as well. Scripture

readings in the synagogue, religious instruction to the young, daily domestic prayers and recitations were all based on the necessity of thorough and systematic exposure to the Bible. The earliest Christians pored over Scripture, devoutly seeking God's word to them. But this devotion to Scripture reading could be distorted.

In the fourth century, hermit monks who had fled to the Egyptian desert to escape the growing worldliness of the Church read the Psalms day by day in cycles of ever-increasing speed. If one monk could get through the Psalms in two weeks, another proved his virtue by doing it in half the time. Eventually the competition had to be stopped. Monks were ruining their health by their ascetic athletics! In this case, Bible texts were not nurturing and disciplining a godly life. Wrong motives were marring the use of the Psalms, and with absurd effects. In a sense, Christians shouldn't try to use the Bible. A better idea is to allow God to use it to illuminate our way through life.

In corporate worship, even when the sequence of readings is carefully prepared, the actual practice of oral congregational reading may have a bad effect. Sometimes when visitors want to join in worship they are put off by an unusual and arbitrary pace of the reading. The visitor's voice may lag behind, or more disastrously, may forge ahead into empty space as the regulars take breath. After one or two tries the visitor lapses into embarrassed and resentful non-participation. Corporate worship? No longer. Instead it has become, at least for the visitor, performance and critical observation.

Preaching Patterns
I attended a church where the pattern of teaching and preaching was carefully laid out for three preaching services each week. On Sunday mornings, a series of sermons on the Psalms was in full swing; in the evenings

they were hearing another series, this time on the epistle to the Romans. Midweek services feature hourlong lectures on the writings of the prophet Isaiah. But the prayers in the services did not reflect concerns for themes such as healing and justice which were central to the prophetic and pastoral Scriptures they had just heard so fully expounded. No time was allowed for reflection on the biblical teaching so that the spirit might have a chance to probe or inspire people on everyday matters. The leaders of this church had developed one of the most comprehensive schemes of Scripture teaching that one could imagine. The Bible was central, but the worship was severely unbalanced. It was top-heavy with head knowledge.

Another approach was used by Mennonites of past generations. Concerned to present the full sweep of the Bible story, they didn't risk leaving anything out. Sunday after Sunday the sermons began with the Garden of Eden and jogged apace right through to the Holy City of Revelation chapter 21. Marathons indeed! People could do no more than wait and wilt as captive listeners through these virtuosic, but droning sermons.

Churches have tried many different patterns. The ways of the hermit monks and the Mennonite preachers had severe drawbacks. But let's look at some other ways, and perhaps we will find more positive examples and possibilities.

In many churches one can hear a series of sermons extending over weeks or months on individual books of the Bible, or on biblical themes such as 'families of the Bible', 'what does it mean to be the church?', or 'lives of great women of the Bible'. Such topics probably represent pastoral concern for areas of the church's life that are weak and need specific nurture. The choice of themes comes from problems of life, and then those problems determine the specific parts of Scripture chosen as the basis for the public worship in the congregation. Congregational worship needs to incorporate a breadth of Scripture which connects with the inevitable breadth of experience of a group of people in any given week of their lives.

Yet another way of choosing Scripture for services is through a board of preachers. Each preacher chooses the topics or passages for the particular services assigned. The spirit will inspire the right theme for the congregation to hear. Each preacher will speak out of the insights that God gives at that time. A church with a number of good preachers will gain wide perspective through this method. The danger is that the biblical diet of the church can be fragmented, distorted, and confused.

Favourite Texts and Biblical Alleyways
Witless repetition, exclusion of visitors through strange liturgical mechanics, over-braininess, fragmentation, confusion – these are some of the difficulties Christians have experienced in attempting to incorporate Scripture in public worship. But the problems can be more than mere weaknesses; they can be actual pitfalls.

The *Favourite Text* is a pitfall well known to Christians individually in our private devotions. As in many of life's difficulties, one aspect of the pitfall is actually a strength. The 'life text' may remind us of a biblical theme that is truly vital. But we distort this when we fix on that one thing while ignoring others which are just as vital. A particular psalm, a life-changing chapter from Romans or certain parables of Jesus to which we return again and again, can become in effect a tiny little Bible if we forget to expose ourselves to the broad sweep of Bible concerns.

Churches have a similar tendency to tread well-worn Bible paths. In a sense this is good, because it can clearly mark the character of the church. Visitors catch certain themes coming repeatedly through the worship. One frequent visitor to our church told us that our major themes were the kindness and goodness of God, though we had not explicitly intended this. This remark, meant as a compliment, made us want to look carefully at our worship to be sure we were not limiting ourselves to partial insights, however comforting and glorious they might be.

Another pitfall is the *biblical alleyway* – high walled, narrow passageways providing us only limited biblical perspectives. Jim Wallis, leader of the Sojourners Community in Washington, DC, illustrates this point dramatically with his 'rich man's Bible'. Jim, while a theological student, took scissors to a Bible and cut out every single reference to the justice and to God's special concern for poor people. When he holds this tattered Bible aloft, it flutters limply, a pathetic, emaciated fragment. By feeding on only a limited number of favourite texts we are heading into a familiar, but limiting pathway. We are in effect cutting ourselves off from the possibility of theSpirit's bringing insight from the entire biblical message.

C. Using the Bible – Principles

Keep the Whole Bible Together
In the stories of certain church leaders branded as heretics and cast out of the ecclesiastical mainstream, we can see how the early church struggled to keep the whole biblical story together. Some of these heretics chose to discount Old Testament passages, claiming that the God of the Old Testament was not the same as the Father of Jesus the Messiah. Others wanted to eliminate New Testament passages that proved the human element in Jesus' life – his real human birth, suffering and death. Just as the early Christians, we must be careful in our determination to retain the message of the whole Bible.

'Vain repetitions!' This put-down has been wielded by those who have ignored or refused the strengths of liturgical worship. They have perhaps observed a priest

'saying the service' at breakneck speed, slowing down
only for those few words '. . . trouble, sorrow, need,
sickness, or any other adversity'. It is easy to retaliate
against this with counter-accusations, but careful reflection enables all of us to understand the complaint
against set prayers, repeated readings of psalms and
other Scripture passages. Of course there is immeasur-
able good in permeating our memories with the words
and phrases of Bible writers, of holy ones through the
ages. And of course we should never allow our minds
and feelings to get disengaged from the reality behind
the familiar words, no matter how often we go over
them. There is no doubt, however, that in repetitious
prayers and readings there is the 'pitfall of vanity'.

Reflect the Theology of our Tradition
When we choose Bible texts, Bible passages for
teaching, and Bible prayers, all of us are guided –
whether we know it or not – by certain principles. It is
important to examine those principles, and to be sure
they are strong ones. We have to make choices: Do we
include this? Then something else must be left out. Our
choices reveal our tendencies and our bias. We will
emphasise what has been important to us and to our
particular church's tradition, even if, as some protest, it
is of no tradition at all – purely independent.

For example, one of the main liturgical churches has
developed a series of Sunday readings organising the
calendar year into three sections of four months each.
The activity of one of the persons of the Holy Trinity is
the theme for each four-month segment. Christmas to
Easter/Pentecost is the period concerned with the Son;
Pentecost through summer is devoted to the work of
the Holy Spirit; and the autumn centres around the
person of the Father in creation and provision for
redemption. What does this scheme reveal about the
church which uses it? It is obviously a church which
remembers its history of needing to formulate and

defend a strongly trinitarian doctrine. If we examine other parts of its liturgy we can see that this emphasis on the Trinity runs through many parts of its worship from week to week. The members of this church feel content with a scheme which in its largest shape and in its smallest detail emphasises trinitarian doctrine.

The powerful memory and model of liberation in the Exodus story impels Christians in the burgeoning 'base communities' around the world. The apostle Paul's metaphor of the Church as the body of Christ provides fundamental inspiration for others, reflected in their songs and sermons. Further examples of powerful metaphors or controlling ideas are the 'household of God', and the 'walk of faith'.

Recognise our Bias

Whatever framework of biblical use that we devise, we reveal our tendencies and our history. No matter how much we may determine to be comprehensive or objective, our own special emphases will become obvious. They will show up in the small details and also in the general patterns. Bias is inevitable. And it is not necessarily bad. Bias is likely to become bad, however, if it is unrecognised. It may then rule instead of serve. It is important to look for and to understand bias, both in ourselves and in others.

In a time of ecumenical idealism, some would say that it would surely be the simplest and most charitable thing for all Christian denominations to agree on a common lectionary, an identical biblical framework for worship and prayers. In a time when the world is looking to the churches for a unified voice, this would seem to be a gesture of solidarity.

But if we simply decide to use another church's lectionary – or the product of a committee of liturgical bureaucrats – it would be like borrowing another family's picture album to put on our living room coffee table. Perhaps their family and our family both spent summer holidays in Cornwall. We might well have looked at the same scenery and bathed on the same beaches. But looking at another family's pictures we see it all from their point of view. We want a photo album that records and reflects our own family's experiences. Both albums have true pictures of Cornwall in the summer, but the truth is big enough to be received from differing perspectives.

In just that way, the Bible is a broad enough panorama to be capable of different series of snapshots. No one set of photos will ever comprehend the whole; but each series will be able to reflect the truth of the pilgrimage of a particular church family. It will help them in their attempt to remember the acts of God and to listen as he communicates his love, justice and plan for a renewed creation.

D. The Courage to Edit

Now we will take a detailed look at how the Bible shapes our worship. Are there new ways for the Bible words to infuse all aspects of our worship – particularly our corporate prayers? I am convinced that there are ways that can help us to make better use of the Bible's actual words as we worship. And these will pose further questions for us.

Dare we 'tamper' with sacred words? Which versions and translations should we choose for public reading? Are there ways of working with the texts, through judicious selecting and editing, that will clarify their message? Each of us will come to different answers to these questions. But as we face them, there is hope that the worship of each of our churches – in its own distinctive way – can become more Bible-centred.

Which Version?
Everyone has a favourite version of the Bible. The verses we memorised as children are truly 'hidden in

the heart'. I remember a worship service primarily attended by older people in which the worship leader called for a congregational recitation of Psalm 1. It was beautiful to see the joy in their faces, and the confidence in their voices as the people recited the well-loved poem together. They never tripped over words like 'walketh', 'standeth', 'sitteth', and 'dost'. They were completely at home with the Authorised Version. It was 'their' Bible.

But it wasn't mine. All those old words were tongue-twisters, and the language sounded terribly archaic. I know Bible verses best in the RSV. But to people younger than me, my quotations must sound archaic!

What a richness we have in the variety of English translations! At the same time the choice can cause arguments and problems. Churches have to make hard decisions when they buy sets of pew Bibles or decide which version to preach from. Which is the most familiar? Which is theologically best? Which has the simplest vocabulary?

Our question here is not which version we use in private or at home. It is which version we choose for public reading. For our purpose, the most important factor is simplicity of language.

Widely accepted, the NIV is an obvious choice for many churches. But the TEV serves equally well for public reading. The words are simple, and the sentences are brief – two factors which help ordinary people to read clearly.

Read the passage aloud, and it quickly becomes clear which is a good version for the purpose. If you want people to understand the text as well as hear it, then choose the one with short sentences and simple words.

Plain Scripture

Once we have chosen our version, we then have to decide how many verses to read. Usually, we decide to go for the whole thing (unless it's Psalm 119!). Who are we to decide to omit a paragraph? If it wasn't too long for the sons of Korah, it can't be too long for us. Longer passages of narrative are manageable, and can be left as they stand. But sometimes it works well to summarise at least a part of the story, either before beginning to read, or in mid-stream.

Most difficult of all are dense passages of complex ideas, like some chapters in Romans or Hebrews. Long readings of such material are counter-productive. After a complex reading people may remember only the last verse they've heard or a favourite verse which might have been a part of the passage. A brief introduction to the passage can alert listeners to the ideas coming up.

Does it seem presumptuous to introduce or summarise a biblical idea in conjunction with a reading? Why are we so reluctant to abbreviate a Bible text? Our reticence may grow out of our reverence for the text. This is entirely proper. But we may hesitate simply because we do not know how to go about choosing and arranging Scriptures for public reading.

'Plain' Scripture, of course, comes to us in forms which are the result of the work editors have done centuries ago. The order of Psalms, sequences of stories and sayings, and divisions into chapters and verses are evidence that human hands were at work with the inspired materials.

Dare to be a Mary

But can we ourselves change Scripture around, leaving out verses, or repeating others out of order? Do we have the privilege of editing the Scripture? Within certain limits, yes, we do. In fact, it is essential that we give careful thought and detailed work to the process of preparing Scripture readings for public worship. It is important that there be a stated and shared understanding within the congregation about this process. Clarity, faithfulness to the meanings, and communication are criteria for the work. In making selections and taking care over the public presentation of Scripture we are following in the tradition of the writers and compilers of the Bible, as well as Christian liturgists and devotional writers through the ages.

Mary, the mother of Jesus, was an editor as well as a poet. As a child she had memorised Scripture. Passages from the law, psalms, and the prophets were deeply and safely stored in her mind. The angel's words, 'You have found favour with God', struck her with fear and awe. Terrified and inspired, Mary poured out her song of enlivened nuggets of Scripture (Hab. 3.18; Job 5.11; II Sam. 22.28; and parts of Pss. 34, 35, 89, 98, 103, 107, 111, 147). Out the Bible phrases flowed, but connected in a new way. In her devout response, Mary spoke out new Scripture. The Magnificat was not original. It was all rooted in the longings, the faith, the agonies and the hopes expressed in the Hebrew scriptures Mary knew so well.

But at the same time, the Magnificat was new. It was new because Mary's experience and the words of Scripture joined to produce a poetic prayer unlike any other before it. It was more than the sum of its parts, as a finished custard is different from the individual components – the eggs, the sugar and the milk.

Jesus, too, was a poet. He was an editor as well as a prophet. Steeped in Scripture as his mother before him, he met life and its crises with the potent forces of Scripture, spirit, insight and image. Jesus' Manifesto in Luke chapter 4 is edited Isaiah (chapters 61 and 58). The Greatest Commandment is edited law (Deut. 6.5; Lev. 19.18). Jesus often built his poetic parables on older rabbinic stories. The turns of phrase, the sharp insight were his spirit-inspired genius at work, bringing life and Scripture together in homely and vivid ways.

We are not going to write new Scripture. We are not Mary or Jesus. But we can follow in their steps by saturating our minds with Scripture. We, like them, can be open to allow Scripture in fresh ways to be a smoothed path for our public worship. When we don't know the words to use, one of the ways the spirit provides for our prayers is the way of Bible words.

Who's Talking?

Shortening passages, inserting antiphons, repeating short phrases – all of these can help listeners to hear what is in the reading. How we present the reading, physically, is vitally important, too.

An idea which involves slightly more vigorous editing requires working with what our English teachers called 'the person' or 'point of view' of a sentence. As we read a passage, we can change the 'person' at a few points, in order to allow the psalm to speak for us, corporately, and to address God more directly. Remember, this suggestion is not about translating the Bible. It's about reading aloud and forming Bible words into prayer.

The first thing to do is notice the point of view in a sentence. Simply ask, 'Who's talking?' Here are three examples from the Psalms:

1. *For the Lord is the great God*
the great King above all gods.
In his hand are the depths of the earth
And the mountain peaks belong to him (Ps. 95.3,4).

In the verses above the psalmist is talking about God to someone who is listening. It is an objective report, a factual account about God. These sentences are in third person.

2. *For I am poor and needy*
And my heart is wounded within me.
I fade away like an evening shadow;
I am shaken off like a locust (Ps. 109.22,23).

Here (above) the psalmist speaks in the first person,

89

as 'I', to someone else.

>   3.   *Not to us, O Lord, not to us*
>   *but to your name be the glory,*
>   *because of your love and faithfulness* (Ps. 115.1).

In this passage (above) a group of people are addressing God. 'We' approach 'you' (God). We are the first person (plural) addressing God.

We have observed who is being addressed and who is speaking. Now we can go on to further steps in learning to read and pray through Scripture in public worship. We can now move toward corporate language.

Corporate Language
Let us look first at Psalm 145, the keystone psalm of the Jewish prayerbook. Its praise encompasses great themes: God is the Lord of creation and history. All created beings are dependent upon him. God is just and a generous provider. No psalm is more appropriate to corporate worship than this one.

The psalmist begins by addressing God personally. Then at verse three he seems to be speaking to others about God. In verse 10 he again addresses God directly. Verse 13 shifts back to speaking about God. The psalmist summarises on the personal note: 'My mouth will speak the praise of the Lord.' Finally, he calls on all of creation to join in praises to God.

Small adjustments in the wording can enable the psalm to serve more explicitly as a corporate prayer. Particularly in verses 13 to 19, the psalm can become a more direct and personalised expression. The following setting makes only small changes in person from the NIV translation:

Psalm 145
  1. We will exalt you, our God and King;
       we will praise your name for ever and ever.

90

2. Every day we will praise you
   and extol your name for ever and ever.

3. You are great, O Lord, and most worthy of praise;
   Your greatness no one can fathom.

4. One generation will commend your works to another;
   We will tell of your mighty acts.

5. We will speak of the glorious splendour of your majesty,
   and we will meditate on your wonderful works.

6. We will tell of the power of your awesome works,
   and we will proclaim your great deeds.

7. We will celebrate your abundant goodness
   and joyfully sing of your righteousness.

8. Lord, you are gracious and compassionate,
   slow to anger and rich in love.

9. Lord, you are good to all;
   you have compassion on all you have made.

10. All you have made will praise you, O Lord;
    all your saints will extol you.

11. We will tell of the glory of your kingdom
    and speak of your might.

12. So that everyone may know of your mighty acts

and the glorious splendour of your kingdom.

13. Your kingdom is an everlasting kingdom.
    and your dominion endures through all genera-
    tions.

    Lord, you are faithful to all your promises
    and loving toward all you have made.

14. Lord, you uphold all those who fall
    and you lift up all who are bowed down.

15. The eyes of all look to you,
    and you give them their food at the proper time.

16. You open your hand and satisfy the desires
    of every living thing.

17. Lord, you are just in all your ways
    and loving toward all you have made.

18. You are near to all who call on you,
    to all who call on you in truth.

19. You fulfill the desires of those who fear you;
    you hear their cry, and you save them.

21. Our mouths will speak in praise of you, Lord,
    Let every creature praise your holy name for ever
    and ever.

If we incorporate similar changes in the opening
verses of Psalm 63 (see NIV), they can serve as a

beautiful opening prayer for corporate worship. This setting makes only slight modifications to the NIV.

Psalm 63 verses 1 to 5

1. O God, you are our God, earnestly we seek you;
   Our souls thirst for you, our bodies long for you,
   In a dry and weary land where there is no water.

2. We have seen you in the sanctuary
   and beheld your power and your glory.

3. Because your love is better than life,
   our lips will glorify you.

4. We will praise you as long as we live.
   and in your name we will lift up our hands.

5. Our souls will be satisfied as with the richest of foods;
   with singing lips our mouths will praise you.

Inclusive Language

Language can exclude! This came vividly to my mind recently, at a community farewell dinner party for a resident member, Eileen. We were a happy fourteen, squeezed in around a long kitchen table. Eileen, the guest of honour, was flanked by Peter and Will. From her vantage point, Eileen could see only women, eleven of us. 'Well, girls,' she said, 'I'll think of you all as the plane takes off.' Peter grimaced. A few minutes later Eileen did it again. 'Girls, this is such a wonderful send-off. Thanks ever so much.' Will and Peter both made faces. Eileen seemed oblivious to the effect of her happy words upon the men sitting to her right and left.

Did it matter? Surely Peter and Will knew that

Eileen included them in her thanks and appreciation. Of course they understood it. But their grimaces and everyone else's laughter showed that more than understanding was necessary. To feel included in Eileen's happy thanks (and unintentional exclusion), Peter and Will had to think a second thought and make an internal translation.

The same kind of thing happens to women in public worship. Yes, we can do the somersault of thought, imputing harmless motives, reassuring ourselves that, grammatically, 'sons' can be made to include 'daughters'. 'Brothers' can be made to mean 'sisters' as well. But by a few, very simple editorial shifts we can allow a Scripture reading to include everyone immediately. And in doing this we do not distort the meaning of the passage at all. We are not translating. We are reading and praying through the words of Scripture, allowing them to lead us, and not to block us.

Don't be deceived, my dear brothers (Add 'and sisters'). Every good and perfect gift . . . (Jas. 1.16).

Those who are led by the spirit of God are sons (substitute 'children') of God (Romans 8.14).

Blessed are the peacemakers for they will be called sons (substitute 'children') of God (Matt. 5.9).

This kind of editing requires care and discretion. Readers must prepare their readings. Not every male pronoun should be changed. Sometimes, in fact, the male pronoun is specific and required: 'I declare to every man who lets himself be circumcised that he is obligated . . . (Gal. 5.3).

But sometimes translators have made choices which reveal a bias towards men in a completely unnecessary way. For example, the NIV translates a phrase in Romans chapter 8, verse 15, '. . . . you received the spirit of sonship'. The translators suggest 'spirit of adoption' only in the footnote to this verse. But the Greek word *huiothesia* means – literally, simply and clearly – 'adoption'. If the editors had cared about the exclusion caused by 'sonship', they could easily have chosen to use 'adoption' in the body of the text. It would in no way have denied the true meaning of the passage.

Occasionally, in a meeting of women only, I have read 'Blessed are the peacemakers, for they will be called daughters of God.' Does this violate the text? No. Does it help Jesus' meaning to become personal to the women present? Yes.

The question of inclusive language in our public worship, prayers and sermons, is not 'cranky'. It is not an issue which might go away if we ignore it. It is a matter of choice, a chance for growth and an exercise of love. We choose the words we use. But once we've chosen them, they shape us. Our words can shield us from growth, or they can help us grow. Let us be careful in our consideration of inclusive language. In everyday conversation we can be sensitive to this question. In writing for publication we can deliberately choose, as I have tried to do in this book, to use 'he' and 'she' interchangeably whenever that is possible. Not least of all, in our worship, inclusive language can lead us to be more sensitive and loving towards all who are present.

Direct Address

Earlier we have observed who is talking in a given Bible passage, noticing the 'I', the 'you', and the 'they' words. In this section we will find ways to construct prayers which address God directly, using words of specific passages. This technique enables intensely personal prayers to emerge.

The final verses of Psalm 91 read almost like a letter from God written to someone about a third person. We look first at the version as it stands in the NIV:

Psalm 91 verses 14 to 16
14. Because he loves me, says the Lord,
     I will deliver him;
   I will protect him,
     for he acknowledges my name.

15. He will call upon me
     and I will answer him;
   I will be with him in trouble,
     I will deliver him and honour him.

16. With long life will I satisfy him,
     and show him my salvation.

   In private prayer, it might be appropriate to person-
alise these verses and hear God speaking directly to
me through the poetry. But notice that with this change
in perspective the revised setting can be suitable for a
group at prayer as well as for an individual praying
alone. This is because in English the word 'you' can be
either singular or plural.

The Lord says:
14. Because you love me,
     I will deliver you;
   I will protect you,
     Because you acknowledge my name.

15. When you call upon me
     I will answer you;
   I will be with you in trouble,
     I will deliver you and honour you.

16. With long life I will satisfy you,

and show you my salvation.

We can also form the psalm verses into a corporate prayer of praise to God, because of the promises expressed in the text:

Thank you, Lord, for your promises to us, that
14. when we love you,
        you will deliver us;
     that you will protect us
        because we acknowledge your name.

Thank you for your promise to us that
15. when we call to you,
        you will answer us;
     you will be with us in trouble,
        you will deliver us and honour us.

Thank you for the promise you have given us that
16. you will satisfy us with long life,
        and show us your salvation.

This psalm portion can also become a prayer of confident resolve in times of trouble:

14. Lord, we love you,
        for we know you will deliver us.
     We seek to acknowledge your name.
        for we crave your protection.

15. Lord, we call to you.
        We know you will answer us.
     We know you are with us in our trouble;
        You will deliver us and honour us.

16. Lord, we receive the life which is your gift to us;
        and we praise you for your salvation.

Justifiable Changes?

Do we have the right to alter the Bible's pronouns? Are these changes legitimate? Let's go back to the purpose of reading Scripture in public worship. We want the words to come alive; we want the spirit to communicate personally and directly through words. The words themselves are not sacrosanct. They are, after all, already translations. It is up to us to open ourselves and be flexible, allow the creative spirit to communicate through the words, bringing them alive.

Yes, there was a reason why the poet chose the 'I' and 'me' forms rather than the 'you' or 'he' forms. And if we were preparing written translations from the original language we would make every effort to write down every detail faithfully. But when we read these psalms as prayers in public worship we are not writing translations. We are praying through the words, keeping our thoughts within the sequence of the original poem. Often, people in the congregation will hear the psalmist's ideas in a fresh way. They will be drawn back to the psalms and hear them as intensely personal prayers. This is one of a number of ways to help the psalms come alive for us. In view of how dry or cliché-ridden our prayer language is, isn't it worthwhile – at least sometimes – to let Bible words be the substance of our prayers?

Praying from the Text

This technique doesn't only work with psalms. Let's turn to several New Testament passages and explore some ways of praying through Bible words.

First of all, a passage from Ephesians:

Ephesians chapter 3 verses 14 to 21
14. I kneel before the Father

98

15. from whom his whole family in heaven and on earth derives its name.

16. I pray that out of his glorious riches
    he may strengthen you with power
    through his Spirit in your inner being.

17. so that Christ may dwell in your hearts through faith;
    And I pray that you, being rooted and established in love,

18. may have power together with all the saints
    to grasp how wide and long and high and deep,
    is the love of Christ,

19. and to know this love that surpasses knowledge,
    – that you may be filled to the measure of all the fullness of God.

20. Now to him who is able to do immeasurably more
    than all we ask or imagine,
    according to his power that is at work within us

21. To him be glory in the church and in Christ Jesus
    throughout all generations, for ever and ever!
    Amen.

It is important to understand how the words are working in our passage. This requires understanding the grammar. Here is one way to do it: Underline the verbs (action words) and circle the pronouns (personal words). In verses 14 to 19, Paul tells the Christians in Ephesus about his prayer for them. As it stands, these verses are not actually a present prayer, but are an account of a past prayer. By means of a few simple changes in verb tenses, however, we can recast the words of this passage so that we have a more immediate prayer, appropriate, for example in the opening of corporate worship.

14. Father, we kneel before you, from whom

15. every family in heaven and on earth derives its name.

16. Father, the riches of your glory are the source of your gifts of grace to us. Grant us, we pray, that we be strengthened with power through your Spirit in our inner being.

17. In our worship, we pray that you, Christ Jesus, may dwell in our hearts through faith. We pray that we may more fully know your love.

21. Father, be glorified in your church and in Christ Jesus now and forever. Amen

These verses could also be used as part of a prayer of intercession. Or they could be incorporated into a service of commissioning for a person or a special working group within the church.

16. Lord, according to the riches of your glory, give strength to (these people) by the power of your Spirit. Encourage and renew them in their inner being.

17. Lord Christ, you dwell in their hearts by faith.

Keep them always grounded in your love.

19. May they know your love which surpasses knowledge, and may they be filled with the fullness of God.

Extempore Prayers
This technique can also help us prepare for leading extempore prayers. Though the prayers are not fully written out, the sequence of ideas is carefully thought through. Let's look again at Ephesians chapter 3, verses 14 to 21, in the NIV.

After grasping the main ideas of the prayer in the Bible text, we can base our free prayer upon those thoughts. The concerns and petitions of the inspired writer can shape our concerns and petitions. This puts Scripture into direct contact with realities of our everyday situations. Here, verse by verse, is a list of the ideas in our passage.

Ephesians chapter 3:
v.16 grant strength by the spirit.
v.17 that Christ may dwell in hearts
     be rooted and established in love.
v.18 may grasp the immense scope of Christ's love
v.19 may be filled with fullness of God
v.20 God is able to do more than we can ask or imagine
v.21 glory comes to God in the church, in Jesus

A prayer might develop along these lines:

Acknowledging the presence and power of the Spirit when we pray,

101

we confess our weaknesses (in specific ways) in relation to the situation that confronts us.

We petition (v.16) the strength and power of the Spirit so that (v.17) Christ's love will establish and root us in the particular ways this situation requires.

We put our concerns, (v.18) imaginatively, into the scope of Christ's love.

We picture the outcome (v.19) God's full love transforming the situation.

We try to imagine it even better (v.20), beyond our requests and dreams.

Glory can come (v.21) through the church, through Christ.

Similar to the one above, this section of Scripture, from Paul's letter to the Philippians includes an embedded prayer for the Church. First, here is the full passage:

Philippians chapter 1, verses 3 to 11 (NIV)
3. I thank my God every time I remember you. 4. In all my prayers for all of you, I always pray with joy 5. because of your partnership in the Gospel from the first day until now, 6. being confident of this, that he who began a good work in you will carry it on to completion until the day of Christ Jesus. 7. It is right for me to feel this way about all of you, since I have you in my heart; for whether I am in chains or defending and confirming the gospel, all of you share in God's grace with me. 8. God can testify how I long for all of you with the affection of Christ Jesus. 9. And this is my prayer: that your love may abound more and more in knowledge and depth of insight, 10. so that you may be able to discern what is best and may be pure and blameless until the day of Christ, 11. filled with the

fruit of righteousness that comes through Jesus Christ –
to the glory and praise of God.

We can lay the foundations for a prayer based on this
passage by first listing, verse by verse, an outline of the
ideas:

3. I thank God . . . for you
4. my prayer . . . is joy
5. thanks for partnership in gospel
6. God began a good work in you
    God will complete it.
7. I hold you . . . in my heart
    we share grace for prison, defence, confirmation of
    the gospel.
8. I long for you
    with affection which is of Christ Jesus
9. My prayer for you:
    your love may abound
    love with more knowledge
    love with deeper insight
10. so that you discern what is best
    so that you be pure, blameless
11. you be filled with fruit of righteousness
    that fruit comes through Jesus Christ.
    Its purpose . . . glory and praise of God.

Before drafting a prayer based on this passage, we
could meditate on experiences we have shared with the
group or the person we are praying for. These
memories which brought joy and thankfulness for the
person could start us off on our prayer. We could
remember how the 'good work' was begun, and recall
the dream for its completion. Confidence in God's
honouring the work could conclude the first section of
the prayer (at v.6).

Verse 7 recalls hard times together, specific struggles

or conflicts, through which we were held together in the unity and sharing (*koinonia*) of the gospel. Out of that hardship has grown a deepened longing and affection which is a gift of Christ Jesus.

Specific petitions will follow. As we meditate on the six requests (vv. 9–11) in the Bible prayer, our deepest hopes for the person will surface. In the reality of the situation, how can love grow and spill over? Where will love that is thoughtful, tough, and clear-sighted do its creative work? What are the needs for the Spirit's prompting, the testing and proving to find what is excellent, what is best in the work ahead? Preparation for leading prayers requires time for silence. Confidently allot time in your meditation for listening time for allowing your intuitive imagination to work. Give the Spirit of God a chance to help you prepare this prayer.

In the words 'so that', verse 10 signals the goal or outcome you desire for the person or group. Notice the purity and single-mindedness in Christ Jesus, which will shine when the work and the motive are brought to the light of the 'day of Christ'.

A rush of biblical texts comes to mind at the mention of 'fruit of righteousness' (v.11). To conclude this beautiful prayer, we can meditate on parallel passages such as:

Matt. 5.16 'see good works and glorify the Father'
John 15.5 'abide in me . . . bear fruit'
Eph. 5.9 'fruit of light – good, right, true'
Jas. 3.18 'harvest of righteousness . . . peace'

The passage closes (v.11b) with the overarching purpose: the praise and glory of God. Try to rephrase that expression, making it specific to the person and situation. You could shape a simple benediction from a verse of the following chapter: 'The peace of God, which transcends all understanding, will guard your hearts and minds in Christ Jesus' (Phil. 4.7).

One could give many examples of Bible passages which can help us to pray using this technique. Let us consider one more. Using James chapter 3, verses 17 and 18, we can make a simple outline of the ideas, then cast the written-out or free prayer in any one of several ways:

James chapter 3, verses 17 and 18 (TEV)

17. But the wisdom that comes from heaven is first of all pure; then peaceloving, considerate, submissive, full of mercy and good fruit, impartial and sincere.
18. Peacemakers who sow in peace raise a harvest of righteousness.

Here is an outline of ideas in the passage:

Wisdom from above is:
   pure
   peaceloving
   considerate
   submissive
   full of mercy
   full of good fruit
   impartial
   sincere
Righteousness is the harvest
   sown in peace
   sown by peacemakers

The richness of ideas in the original language shows up if we use other translations to make a list of qualities of wisdom. For example, TEV yields this list: Wisdom from above is pure, peaceful, gentle, friendly, full of compassion, producing good deeds, and free of prejudice and hypocrisy.

This passage could be shaped into parallel lists. On one side, qualities seen in Jesus, with allusions to incidents in his ministry which reveal those qualities; on the other side, a petition to God that these qualities may mark us, his disciples today.

Another development of this passage would be to use the picture of peacemakers sowing seeds and looking for the harvest. The harvest would include qualities of justice and goodness (v.17). One might form a mental picture of Jesus, the wisdom of God in person, sowing seeds in us. The seeds of purity, peace, mercy and sincerity germinate and send out sprouts of justice in our lives. Eventually God, the big shalom maker, comes to bring in the harvest. Biblical 'shalom' (wholeness) in all areas of life is God's creation intention.

Lord's Prayer, an Outline Prayer

From earliest times to our own, no prayer has been more commonly used among Christians than this one. But in the early days they didn't simply repeat it as we usually do. In the writing of the second century North African teacher, Tertullian, we find evidence that in Carthage, and elsewhere in the early Christian churches, it was not simply recited as we have it recorded in the gospels. Instead, it served these Christians as a kind of 'superstructure', a pattern prayer, People could extemporise around the basic lines of the prayer.[17]

This method of praying through the treasured words is still useful. The following is a possible way to develop the prayer in a reasonably small group. It can be divided into five sections and written out on a large sheet of paper, with gaps between the sections. Along the sides are headings for specific concerns. Before the prayer, people could offer specific items to fill in the spaces under the headings. The prayer leader then could point to the phrases of the Lord's Prayer, each in turn, indicating that all can say the words together. But before each new phrase of the Lord's Prayer, the leader would add the concerns which have been written under the appropriate heading. A musical setting of the Lord's Prayer could conclude.

THE LORD'S PRAYER

(Words of the prayer)   (Headings for concerns)

Our Father in heaven   PRAISE
Hallowed be your name.

Your kingdom come   THE CHURCH AND THE WORLD
Your will be done   PEACE, JUSTICE, WHOLENESS

on earth as in heaven.

Give us today our daily bread.   PROVISION OF OUR NEEDS

Forgive us our sins as we forgive   CONFESSION
those who sin against us.

Do not bring us to the time of   PROTECTION FROM EVIL
trial but deliver us from evil.

For yours is the kingdom, the   GLORY TO GOD!
power and the glory for ever.

Getting about in the Bible
To use the Bible in prayer it is important to develop the skill of finding your way around in it. Parallel versions of gospel stories and texts with similar themes can illuminate meditation and enrich the preparation of prayers.

The most accessible tools are concordances at the back and references in the margins of study Bibles. It is surprising how many people never notice these helps. Using them can be like going on a treasure hunt of meanings, chasing up related ideas through different books of the Bible. More detailed help comes in larger concordances and lexicons. Every house group interested in studying the Bible should have at least one concordance, Bible dictionary, and lexicon for the use of the members. Worship leaders, too, will find such books helpful in preparing scriptural frameworks for prayers and meditations.

Probing the Meanings
Don't let the variations in English translations annoy or intimidate you. Use the variety to learn more about the meanings behind the words. If you read and then copy out your chosen verses in varying translations you will realise that the translators have had to make choices. There are many differences that seem significant. This may be because the original text was unclear. Or a particular aspect of the biblical language may have no direct parallel in our language. Choices may even be based on a policy such as the one adopted by the Bible Society in producing the TEV. The translators have chosen a limited vocabulary, common usage and short sentences. They have presented the text in a clean layout with simple pictures. But more significantly, the differences in translation may reveal the translators' bias.

James chapter 13 verse 18, offers a good example of the variety of meanings that translators give us.

The harvest of righteousness is sown in peace by those who make peace. (RSV)
Peacemakers who sow in peace raise a harvest of righteousness. (NIV)
Goodness is the harvest that is produced from the

seeds the peacemakers plant in peace. (TEV)

Peacemakers, when they work for peace, sow the seeds which will bear fruit in holiness. (JB)

The peacemakers go on quietly sowing for a harvest of righteousness. (Phillips)

True justice is the harvest reaped by peacemakers from seeds sown in a spirit of peace. (NEB)

For one Greek word, *dikaiosune*, the translators have chosen from among four English words 'justice', 'holiness', 'righteousness' and 'goodness'. Even the order of words in the sentence can reveal a difference in importance, or emphasis in meaning. What is mentioned first – the peacemakers, or the fruit of the harvest? Our various versions of the Bible are filled up, literally verse by verse, with the editorial decisions of the Bible translators. This is why it is useful and illuminating to compare versions and to go as deeply as we can in probing the meanings behind our English texts.

The Power of Bible Words

In preparing prayers we always search for the words that work best. Words are powerful tools, more potent than we usually imagine. Words are not like wooden cubes to be pushed through square holes in a child's game. The words we choose have power over our thoughts and perceptions, so we must handle our language with care.

When we survey different translations, a respect for language helps us to realise that an original meaning was bigger or more complicated than any single phrase or word in a translation can convey. We can see that the translators have had to struggle to express a reality that will approximate that of the original text.

Similarly, our prayers must stretch for the right words. They must encompass more than one expression of an idea. By using tools of Bible study, using different

109

translations, developing our imaginations and using our mental picture-making abilities we can enrich and broaden our corporate prayers.

Praying in our own words, extempore, is good. But we must be careful not to fall into habits of using worn-out or debased words. There are no biblical models for the 'just now, O Lord, . . .' prayer, or for the 'lead, guide and direct' tautology. The best way to avoid getting into ruts and repetition in our prayers is to feed our minds on Bible words. The Bible will give strong structure and sensible meaning to our prayers. Preparing public prayers for church services isn't easy. It requires gift, imagination, and a strong commitment of time and mental energy. But when we are willing to grow and change, how fruitful the results can be – for all of God's people.

For Thought and Action

Observe how the Bible is used in your worship – patterns of readings, sermon series. Is there a corporate approach?

Does your church run in a biblical alleyway? What are its confines? How can you take precautions against the dangers?

How is the theology of your church's tradition reflected in your worship?

Can you put additional Bible aids into your church library and show people how to use them? Teach New Testament Greek in the local church?

How can you sharpen awareness of inclusive language? First listen to the hurt, then decide if it's worth making adjustments in public language.

Getting practice:
– Write your own paraphrases after looking at several translations of a particular passage.
–Set a passage for several readers: e.g., Hebrews 11; Romans 8.
– Write a dramatic setting of a narrative: e.g., Joshua chapter 4, verses 1 to 7, stories from Nehemiah
– Write your own psalms, working in a selection of Scriptures that surround your life story.
– Look again at Psalm 167, verses 42, 43, and 67 to observe the built-in antiphons. Choose another psalm, choose an antiphon verse, write out the psalm as a reading for a combination of readers and congregation.
– Try out Psalm 145 in corporate language, as a public prayer. Do this with other psalms. Practice on a few friends before using in public worship.

Set up a readers' workshop to help those who read publicly to project their voices, to read expressively and to pace the readings well.

In private prayers, read psalms in direct address. If this enhances your ability to pray through the psalms, work it into public prayers.

In private, develop prayers based on idea-framework of a passage. If this proves useful, try it in leading public prayers.

In a smallish group, use the Lord's Prayer as an outline prayer.

Build up your own collection of versions of the Bible, become alert to variation and carefully choose the version for the particular occasion or purpose.

4: Praise

Praiseworthy and laudable. We seldom find religious words which are still in everyday English conversation and the newspaper, but these two are. 'The success of the schoolchildren in raising £325 for charity is truly praiseworthy.' 'Laudable efforts by conservationists have saved the trees along the new road.'

It is natural and right to acknowledge good when we see it. It gives us pleasure. It is not only appropriate, then, when we praise God, it is necessary. It also satisfies something deep within us. It feels good! Not that we give something we possess, but that we acknowledge the true nature of things. We receive measureless good, and as we turn our faces to the giver, we praise him and say thank you.

Christians almost instinctively begin corporate worship with praise and thanks to God. We move towards God, just as we would take steps to meet any treasured friend. We anticipate the meeting, and our hearts lift as the time approaches.

But our relationship with God is not just like that with a treasured friend. Moving towards an encounter with God is never the same as approaching a social rendezvous. God, the one we meet in worship, is personal, but God is beyond personality. In worship we encounter the one who is unimaginably bigger and more profound than his entire creation. We cannot approach him lightly. But we do approach him as Jesus taught us to, in confidence and within a relationship of mutual love. When we gather for corporate worship we reflect on Jesus' way of prayer, and in doing that we can establish an inner quiet and openness to listen to God.

Christians aren't unique in struggling to find the composure of mind and spirit necessary for worship. The Jews have a special word for this concentrated inward attention and devotion: *kawannah*. It is the attitude in which the inward eyes and heart are directed to God's presence. Jews often prayed with their hands open and stretched upward. One of the rabbis said, 'One's prayer is not accepted unless one puts the heart in the hands.' The hands open and lift to receive good gifts from God.

Inner quiet, anticipation, a thankful spirit: these are all necessary qualities of heart as we approach worship. In reflective moments it is natural to think back over what has recently happened, and this is a useful discipline of mind as we begin worshipping together. When we are especially aware of being in God's presence, all kinds of things come to mind – all the experiences of our lives in which we have known God's mercy, care, protection and provision.

A. Open Worship

Many of our churches have meetings in which there is a time of spontaneity. In this 'open worship' time, people are encouraged to pray, lead a song or speak in an inspired way. These spontaneous periods can be fruitful, but sometimes they are not.

Public, open worship creates a complex situation. People's outward participation depends on many factors: the number of people, the size of the room, the acoustics, leadership style, people's cultural expectations, their personality types.

Some negative factors can be at work, subtly undermining the power of the open times. Pressure to conform to verbal formulas can compel people to speak in certain patterns. This may exclude others. Self-promotion by an unbalanced person, perhaps a visitor, can upset the whole group. Most disturbing of all is the congregation's sense of being manipulated by musicians or by a leader. Resentment is a wet blanket which can put out any worship fire.

But in open worship things can also gel in an exciting way. The Holy Spirit can be the one to set the tone, inspire the contributions, bring the healing, and maintain humility in leadership. So the question simply is: How can we preserve peace and openness, purity and receptivity to the spirit?

One activity noticeably absent in open worship is silence. Listening to God, weighing what has been said, allowing a song to 'sink in', developing a sense of ease – all of these aspects of worship are impossible if a fast pace and verbosity dominate. Members of a congregation can develop habits of remaining quiet at the end of a song, of being at ease with quietness. The worship leader plays a key role in enabling creative silence in worship. If the silence is clearly deliberate, and clearly not an awkward scrambling for who should be filling the gap, people will follow the lead. Everyone can be poised and expectant in the silence.

There are two good reasons why so much has been written on the subject of open or free worship. The first is that people deeply desire spontaneity and freedom in worship. The second is that spontaneity is difficult to handle, and is especially open to distortion. It is no wonder that over and again in the history of the Church, people have given up on spontaneity and chosen the easier way of formula and control.

B. 'Lining Out' a Psalm

The strongest way to open public worship is to use Bible words. Consider the following two examples. In each, an opening section for corporate worship includes a psalm portion, then a short extempore prayer followed by a hymn. These three elements (the psalm, the prayer, and the song) are linked in theme. In each example the psalm establishes a context for worship that is as wide as all creation.

The easiest way to use these readings is for one person to read the psalm, and then pray the prayer. But another good way, which has the advantage of gaining the participation of all people, is to 'line out' the psalm.

This is easy to do. The leader speaks one line, and the congregation says it back in the same inflection and speed as the leader. There is nothing new about this. Many of the older people may remember this antique method. It has a number of strengths. Since people don't have to look down at their Bibles, they can stand for the reading, lifting their faces and feeling physically at ease. All can participate, including children, blind, and non-literate people. Everyone is able to participate better than when simply listening to a reading.

The words of Scripture have more of a chance to sink in because every person present hears them first and then speaks them. Through the repetition we allow twice as much time for the ideas to be absorbed. And when we all say the words out loud together, they can become truly *our* ideas. Don't worry that you present half as many ideas in a given amount of time.

When this method of lining out Scripture is used it is easy for people to participate. Careful preparation by the leader is essential to ensure that people can take part with ease.

Here are a few practical suggestions:

1. Choose a Bible version which uses simple, intelligible vocabulary. The TEV is often best for this. Other versions can serve successfully if the leader divides up the sentences.

2. The Bible passage should not be too long. It may be good to shorten a section by making a selection of

verses. An opening verse may be repeated as a closing for the reading.

3. Write or type out the entire reading, rather than reading it straight out of the Bible. This ensures that you notice and prepare every word and line.

4. Practice reading it aloud, preferably with a helper to speak back the congregational parts. People will repeat not only the words, but also the speed, inflection and emphasis of the words.

5. The leader's eyes are as important as the voice. Look into people's faces when speaking the lines. Experience will prove how vitally important eye contact is!

6. It may help the congregation to have an assistant standing beside the reader, a person who leads the congregation in their repetitions. The verbal directions can then be minimal. The leader may say, 'Please repeat the words of each line after me. (Sarah) will lead you in your response. You will speak with her.' If a few people in the congregation understand how this works, they can, by coming in strongly, also help to lead the response. Having an assistant whom the congregation is watching and following allows the reader to glance down and prepare the upcoming line.

C. Opening with the Bible

Here are two possible ways to open a service. Each one uses the sequence: psalm portion, brief extempore prayer, and song. The psalm portions as written out here work well when lined out by a leader and answered by the congregation.

Reading from Psalm 145

We will extol you, Our God and King,
And bless your name forever.

Every day we will bless you
And praise your name forever.

Lord, you are faithful in all your words.
You are gracious in all your deeds.

Lord, you uphold those who are falling.
You raise up all those who are bowed down.

The eyes of all your creation look to you.
And you give them their food in due season.

You open your hand,
And you satisfy.
You satisfy the desire of every living thing.

Lord, you are fair.
You are just in all your ways.
You are kind in all your doings.

We will extol you, Our God and King.
And bless your name forever.

An extempore prayer following the psalm may build
on the psalmist's ideas. This slows the entrance of ideas
and enables the original text to sink in more deeply.
The speed and tone in the extempore prayer can be
deliberate and meditative. (At the conclusion of the
extempore prayer the leader can bring in some ideas or
actual phrases of the next hymn or song to be sung,
making a natural link.)

A prayer based on the ideas in the psalm

Lord, we praise you! We thank you, Lord, that you
are faithful and gracious. Thank you that you lift us

117

when we are bowed down. Thank you for your open hand of provision. Thank you that you are fair and just and kind. Thank you that you are near to us when we call on you. Thank you that you hear us when we call on you in truth.

Lord, we are here. We come as we are, for there is no other way in which to come. We are not all that we would wish to be. We are your children. We need your care, your healing, your encouragement, your love.

Thank you most of all for Jesus who showed us so beautifully, so perfectly who *you* are. It is in his name that we meet here today.

Great is your faithfulness. All we have needed your hand has provided. We bless you, our God and King. And we praise you forever.

Hymn: Great is thy faithfulness, O God our Father.

Here is another example of a sequence of psalm, prayer and hymn in which, through the method of lining out, the Bible presents ideas that can be heard and spoken by everyone. The prayer and the hymn reinforce the same themes.

Reading from Psalm 104

We will sing to you, Lord, all our life long.
As long as we live we will sing your praises.

May you be pleased with our songs,
For our gladness comes from you.

All of your creation depends on you.
You give us food when we need it.

You provide our food,
And we are satisfied.

When you turn away, we are afraid.
When you take away our breath, we die,
And go back to the dust from which we came.

But you send out your spirit, and we are created.
You give new life to the earth.

We will sing to you, Lord, all our life long.
As long as we live we will sing your praises.

After a pause, the extempore prayer may follow the reading, possibly along these lines. You will note that many of the words and phrases come from this psalm, and also from Psalm 103.

A prayer based on the ideas in the psalm

Lord, we will sing your praises as long as we live. You have given us life, you have loved and cared for us. We thank you. We come together here knowing our weakness and our sin. We thank you that we come to you as children to their parents, for comfort and for forgiveness. We bless you, for you are the one who forgives. You are the one who heals. You are the one who saves us from darkness, who crowns us with love and mercy, who satisfies us with good as long as we live. We bless you, for you are the one who works justice for the weak and the oppressed. We bless you, for you are merciful and gracious, slow to anger, and abounding in steadfast love. Accept our worship and our love.

Hymn: O Bless the Lord, my soul.

Here is another way to open a worship service, one which uses Bible words and involves the whole congregation. This reading calls for the congregation's words to appear on an overhead screen, wall sheet or banner. It is short and simple: 'Holy, holy is the Lord!' The

119

reading requires two people to lead. One person will read the main Scripture portion. The other will strongly say the words: 'And so we shout . . .' which bring the people in with their words: 'Holy, holy is the Lord.'

Reading from Isaiah 11 and 12 and Luke chapter 1

With joy we draw water from the wells of salvation.
We give thanks to you, our God.
We call on your name.
We will make known your deeds among the nations
And proclaim that your name is exalted!

And so we shout: HOLY, HOLY IS THE LORD!

Our God judges the wretched with integrity
And with equity gives a verdict for the poor of the land.
God puts down the mighty from their thrones
And exalts those of low degree.
God fills the hungry with good things
And sends the rich empty away.

And so we shout: HOLY, HOLY IS THE LORD!

In all of God's holy mountain
There shall be neither hurt nor destruction.
For the earth shall be full of the knowledge of God
As the waters cover the sea.

And so we shout: HOLY, HOLY IS THE LORD!

D. Wide Horizons in Prayer

An Opening Prayer

Christians in the early centuries believed that they had been drawn into a cosmic plan. They had a place in God's big design for history. Even though they were often only small groups of believers, and in many places were actually persecuted, their prayers did not convey timidity or discouragement. Quite the opposite.

Look at this prayer from fourth-century Christians in Syria. It was based on a form of Jewish prayers and so it has the character of Old Testament poetry. Notice not only the inclusion of historic and even cosmic themes but also an intensely personal spirit. The tone is joyous, full of wonder at God's goodness. We may not choose to use exactly this prayer in our worship. But it reminds us of the immense scope and inclusiveness of Christian worship. Perhaps this prayer can stimulate us to widen our public prayers, to include historical as well as modern and personal concerns.

We give you thanks for all things, O Blessed God,
that you have never removed your kindness and mercy from us.

But in every generation you have saved, delivered, assisted and protected.
    You assisted in the days of Enos and Enoch,
    In the days of Moses and Joshua,
    In the days of Samuel and the judges,
    In the days of Elijah and the prophets,
    In the days of David and the kings,
    In the days of Judith,
    In the days of Judas Maccabaeus and his brothers.

And in the latter days you have assisted us
By your great High Priest, Jesus, who is the Christ, your only Son.

    He has delivered us from the sword.
    He has freed us from famine and sustained us.
    He has delivered us from sickness.
    He has preserved us from an evil tongue.

For all these things we give you thanks through Jesus
Christ.
You have given us an articulate voice to confess.
And added to it a suitable tongue as an instrument to
modulate.
You have given us a proper taste, and a suitable
touch,
A sight for contemplation,
And hearing for sounds.
You have given us smelling for the smelling of
vapours,
Hands for work and feet for walking.

And all these members you form from a little drop in
the womb.
And after the formation you bestow upon it a soul,
And produce it into the light as a rational creature.

You have instructed us by your laws.
You have improved us by your statutes.
And when there comes a dissolution for a while,
You have promised us a resurrection!

Therefore, what life is sufficient,
What length of ages will be long enough for us to be
thankful?

To do it worthily is impossible.
But to do it according to our ability is just and right.

You sent Jesus the Christ among us, being the only
begotten Son.
You made the Comforter to inhabit among us.
You set the angels over us.
You put the devil to shame.
You brought us into being when we were not.
You took care of us when we were made.
You measure out our life to us.

You afford us our food.

Glory and worship be to you for all these things,
Through Jesus Christ,
Now and forever, through all the ages to come![18]

A Poem of Praise
The following text comes from the earliest known
Christian book of songs. These second-century songs
are called 'Odes of Solomon'. Who was the Solomon in
the title? It remains a mystery. This ode is reminiscent
of a psalm, so we could call it a 'new psalm' in the
tradition of the Magnificat. Just as Mary's response to
the angel's announcement was filled with scriptural
allusion, so this author has also been inspired. It shares
with other early Christian writings an expression of
faith which is both cosmic and personal.

Odes of Solomon 16

As the work of the husbandman is the ploughshare;
> And the work of the steersman is the guidance of
> the ship:
So also my work is the Psalm of the Lord;
> My craft and my occupation are in his praises;
Because his love hath nourished my heart,
> And even to my lips his fruits he poured out.
For my love is the Lord
> And therefore I will sing unto him.
For I am made strong in his praise.
> And I have faith in him.
I will open my mouth
> And his spirit will utter in me
The glory of the Lord and his beauty;
> The work of his hands and the fabric of his fingers;
The multitude of his mercies,
> And the strength of his Word.
For the word of the Lord searches out the unseen thing

And scrutinises his thought.
For his eye sees his works,
    And the ear hears his thought.
It is he who spread out the earth,
    And settled the waters in the sea:
He expanded the heavens,
    And fixed the stars;
He fixed the creation and set it up . . . (11 lines lost)
And there is nothing that is without the Lord;
    For he was before any thing came into being.
And the worlds were made by his Word.
    And by the thought of his heart.
Glory and honour to his name.
Hallelujah.[19]

For Thought and Action

What factors inhibit or encourage people to participate in 'open worship' in our church?

How can we encourage freedom in participation, and at the same time prevent distortions to the quality of peace and poise that we may value in our worship?

Can we learn to feel at ease with silence, to view it as a positive quality in worship, in which we listen inwardly to the spirit?

We can enrich open worship with stories of God's action in our own lives. How can we keep these stories lively and specific?

How can we widen our scope of praise?

    Incorporate songs and hymns from other countries.

    Visual symbols remind us of natural creation

Tell our own stories of the week.

Expect to bring evidences of God at work.

'Count your blessings, name them one by one.'

Bring stories from Christians in other places.

5: Confession

'I can see that you confess your faith. But whenever do you confess your sins?' My Catholic friend has stepped on my sensitive toe.

I think to myself: What right does she have to imply that I don't confess my sins? Of course I do. My Protestant reflex is to say that I don't need a priest to intervene on my behalf. I know I have direct access to my advocate with the Father – Jesus Christ, the Just One. He is the atoning sacrifice for my sins. It says so right there in I John chapter 2, verse 1!

So I tell my friend that I know that the Father is faithful and just. He forgives me and cleanses me from all unrighteousness. My sins and my confessions are nobody's business by my own. My emphatic tone of voice stops the conversation: 'Certain prayers are supposed to be private, just between me and God.'

Thinking back on her question and my knee-jerk response, I realised that we were replaying an ancient Catholic/Protestant record. My friend knows what confession is, and she has forms of prayer to express it. But I know what confession is, too, and I know how to pray my penitence.

It is time for a closer look at this worn but wonderful word, confession. It has its place not only in our private prayers, but also in our corporate prayers.

A. Confession: A Two-Edged Word

'Swear by Caesar! Take the oath! Curse Christ! To the lions if you refuse! Do you admit you are a Christian?'

Refusing to be bowed by such taunts and threats, many early Christians firmly declared that they were indeed followers of Jesus. Those who endured persecution and torture, but who were not actually put to death, were called *confessors*. To earn this honoured title one had to have endured terrible suffering and confessed publicly to the crime of being a Christian. That confession revealed one's true identity and absolute loyalty.

Isn't it fascinating that a negative meaning – to admit a fault or a crime – came to take on a positive significance for Christians? The context of persecution made a bad word – confess – into a good word. 'All they that do confess thy holy name,' intones the General Confession in the Book of Common Prayer (1662), and we who declare our belief as Christians, are proud to join in that number.[20]

Confession embraces both the negative and positive meanings. It is a wonderful two-edged word for our worship. 'Confession' can express our belief in God's love, purpose and power, and at the same time it can mean our awareness of our own faults, weaknesses and rebellious nature. A fuller understanding of confession can help Christians to 'take hold of the eternal life to which you were called when you made *the good confession* in the presence of many witnesses, and in the presence of God' (I Tim. 6.12–3).

'We acknowledge and bewail our manifold sins and wickedness, which we, from time to time, most grieviously have committed.' Countless generations of Christians, as they prepared themselves for happier parts of the service, have sighed over these words from the General Confession. After confessing God's creative and just goodness, Christians catalogued and confessed their misdoings, requesting God to forgive and restore. So in this one prayer we find both kinds of confession – a confession of God's power and goodness, and a confession of human sin and weakness.

B: Confession in the Bible

The Psalms

Many psalms show a similar interplay between joy in acknowledging God's steadfast love and penitence for human sin. A well-known example is Psalm No. 51, verses 1 and 2:

> Have mercy on me, O God,
>   according to your unfailing love;
> according to your great compassion
>   blot out my transgressions.
> Wash away all my iniquity
>   and cleanse me from my sin.

We see ourselves as we truly are, only as we raise our eyes to God's goodness. Realising that God's mercy and forgiveness can reach and deliver us, we can only respond with thanksgiving! An outburst of thanks and praise is the most natural conclusion to a confession. We find an almost instinctive pattern for prayer as we move through these three questions – What are we like? What is God like? How do we respond?

The New Testament

There are numerous psalms which combine exalted praise to God along with abject personal confession. But in the New Testament we do not find models of prayer like this. Instead we find long lists of human weaknesses, solid chunks of theology of sin, meditations on Jesus' atoning work which breaks the power of the evil one, and soaring passages celebrating God's unmerited forgiveness. But there are few direct admonitions and models for confession of sin.

There are numerous passages in the New Testament on forgiveness, including Jesus' insight which connects our ability to receive forgiveness to our willingness to forgive others. But there are only two New Testament teachings specifically on *confession*. These appear in I John chapter 1, verse 9, and James chapter 5, verse 16. Neither text is addressed to individual Christians nor advocated as a technique for private devotion. Both are in the context of advice to congregations. Both call for corporate life marked by patience and simplicity (James 5) and by wholeness, peace and justice (I John). The emphasis in both is upon the benefits of the new life in the body of Christ rather than on a catalogue of sins or admonitions to repent.

C: Corporate Confession

The New Testament seems to indicate that we need to discover more fully this corporate perspective. Yes, as individuals we confess and are restored. But the Church as a body needs repentance and healing. The Spirit can inspire forms of prayer to make our corporate consciences sensitive.

Scripture provides a solid base for such prayers. The Spirit inspired the Bible writers in the first place. And Christian experience has shown that these poems, letters and stories can continue to nurture not only individuals, but also churches in their prayers.

There is no need to deprecate the rich veins of confession in churches' history of confession. Liturgical churches have taught and prayed in the traditions of sacramental theologies of confession and absolution. Their prayers and litanies of confession have served generations of faithful Christians.

Non-conformist Christians have similarly taught and practised forms of piety in which personal soul-searching and vulnerability to God's Spirit have borne the fruits of humility and purity in everyday lives. These patterns of piety, formal and informal, have sprung from pastoral insight, from psychological expertise and from biblical sources. They have been responses to the promptings of the Spirit who knows and helps us to express our inner groanings.

The worship materials which follow point to a form of confession which is both corporate and biblical. Through these materials, or others similarly developed, both the liturgical prayers of confession and the extempore prayers of confession more familiar to the Free Churches, can expand in scope.

D. Confession Meditations for Congregations

Your Kingdom Come

What qualities of life does God intend for the Church? The following confession expresses Jesus' and the apostles' deepest desires for Christians, not only as individuals, but also as Christians together.

This reading might have a place in a service celebrating unity. For example, it could be used at a time of reconciliation of estranged members, at a 'birthday' of the congregation or at an annual renewing of covenant.

It could also serve as the basis for more than a prayer or meditation. The reading could provide a framework for brief periods of teaching interspersed among the sections. It would then become an expression of new resolve as well as confession.

Let me say it again, readers must rehearse the reading! There must be careful timing, neither too fast nor too slow, so that the Scripture can sink in. One way to pace the reading is for *Reader B* to repeat silently in her own mind what *Reader A* has just read aloud, before reading aloud her own passage.

YOUR KINGDOM COME!

Reader A: Jesus said: Don't be fearful, little flock, for it is your Father's good pleasure to give you the kingdom. Look! God's reign is evident among you (Luke 12.32; 17.21)!

130

B: *Let us not be anxious about our life.*

A: Our Father in heaven knows that we need all these things: food, clothes and drink (Matt. 6.32).

B: *There are to be no poor among us, because the Father has provided enough for all (Acts 4.34; Deut. 15.4).*

A: Are we tempted to say in our hearts, 'We are rich, we have prospered, we need nothing'? Do we despise the Church of God and humiliate those who have nothing? One's abundance is to supply another's needs, so that there may be equality (Rev. 3.17; I Cor. 11.22; II Cor. 8.15).

B: *There are to be no poor among us.*

ALL: YOUR KINGDOM COME, YOUR WILL BE DONE, ON EARTH AS IT IS IN HEAVEN! (pause)

B: *Let us be people of the truth.*

A: We can recognise what is true, for the Spirit of truth lives among us and is in us. Why then do we allow controversy and disputes about words to spring up among us, disputes which produce the evil fruit of envy, suspicion and dissension (John 14.17; 1 Tim. 6.3–5)?

B: *Let us listen only to the sound words of our Lord Jesus Christ and the teaching which accords with godliness (1 Tim. 6.3).*

A: The spirit has promised to guide us into all truth (John 16.13).

ALL: YOUR KINGDOM COME, YOUR WILL BE DONE, ON EARTH AS IT IS IN HEAVEN! (pause)

B: *Let us come alive in the Spirit who gives life!*

A: The Spirit who raised Jesus from the dead lives in us, and gives life to us (Rom. 8.11).

B: *Does our life give an appearance of vitality, and yet in truth we are comatose? As ones who are asleep? The Spirit says, 'Wake up, and strengthen what remains, which is almost at the point of death' (Rev. 3.1–2).*

131

A: Jesus promised that in his coming we may have life, and have it in full measure (John 10.10).

ALL: YOUR KINGDOM COME, YOUR WILL BE DONE, ON EARTH AS IT IS IN HEAVEN! (pause)

B: *Let us learn patience and endurance.*

A: Think of what Jesus went through, how he put up with such hostility from sinners! Remember his firm profession before Pontius Pilate (Heb. 12; I Tim. 63).

B: *Can we consider it fortunate when all kinds of trials come our way? Have we learned that when our faith succeeds in facing such testing the result will be the ability to endure (James 1.3)?*

A: Jesus said: There will come a time for you to bear testimony. I will give you words and wisdom so that none of your enemies can refute or contradict what you say (Mark 13.9).

B: *By our endurance we will gain life.*

ALL: YOUR KINGDOM COME, YOUR WILL BE DONE, ON EARTH AS IT IS IN HEAVEN! (pause)

B: *Let us learn humility and service.*

A: Let us be of the same mind. Let us have the same love and be in full accord.

B: *Think of the humility of our Lord Jesus, who gave up heavenly honour to become a servant. He took up the task of a servant, and washed his disciples' feet. He said, 'I, your Lord and Teacher have just washed your feet. You, then, should wash one another's feet. I have set an example for you, so that you will do just what I have done for you' (Phil. 2.7; John 13.14).*

A: Why do we resist this teaching, which is so clearly the mind of Christ? Let us have this mind among ourselves, which is ours in Christ Jesus (I Cor. 2.16)!

ALL: YOUR KINGDOM COME, YOUR WILL BE DONE, ON EARTH AS IT IS IN HEAVEN! (pause)

B: *Let us learn to love the world.*

132

A: God so loved, so loved the world. God sent his Son into the world not to condemn the world, but so that the world through him might be saved (John 3.16–7).

B: *Why are we so quick to judge, to condemn our neighbours? Why are we content to ignore and to demean the poor and weak around us? God loves, God sends, God cares, God saves.*

A: Jesus said, 'Be people of mercy, just like your Father, who is merciful' (Luke 6.36).

ALL: YOUR KINGDOM COME, YOUR WILL BE DONE, ON EARTH AS IT IS IN HEAVEN! (pause)

B: *In all of these things, let us seek first the kingdom of God, as Jesus told us to do* (Matt. 6.33).

A: We know that the kingdom of God is not food and drink, but it is justice and peace and joy in the Holy Spirit (Romans 14.17).

B: *Let us then pursue what makes for peace and for mutual upbuilding* (Romans 14.19).

A: And the God of peace will fill us with all joy and peace in believing.

ALL: SO THAT BY THE POWER OF THE HOLY SPIRIT WE MAY SIMPLY OVERFLOW WITH HOPE (Romans 15.13)!

Let Us Walk as Children of Light

When is a confession not a confession? If we don't have the ingredients of 'We're sorry' and 'God has made it right' it may not seem to fit the category. We will see how Jesus and the apostles, without using expected formulas, widen our understanding of confession and forgiveness.

The story of Jesus and the woman taken in adultery will help us to see the point (John 8.2–11). When Jesus first spoke to the woman he did not demand a confession. He asked where her accusers were. Jesus didn't use a formula to pronounce God's love to her and offer an assurance that all was made right again.

But surely this is a story of confession, forgiveness, and resolution. Jesus' own presence of purity and his act of liberating justice made all the difference. Jesus helped the woman to see herself vividly in the light of his goodness and love. With the words 'Go and sin no more' he sent her back into her own life. Jesus had literally delivered her from certain death. He invited her to live a life of purity, and set her face in the right direction. Only Jesus has the authority to make such a call on our lives. Our grateful and obedient reponse to him is an active form of confession.

'Encourage each other', 'practice generous hospitality', 'be merciful' – the challenge is for us to allow these expressions from Scripture (Eph. 4.29; Romans 12.13; Matt. 5.7) to go deep into our consciousness. If we use such expressions over and again in our worship, they will inform our daily actions. Let us provide time in our public prayers for these concerns, these gracious words, to be made our own.

The apostle Paul was a skilful master of what today's psychologists might call positive reinforcement. In passages such as Philippians Chapter 1, he says to his friends, in effect: 'I can see good things happening among you and I want to encourage you to keep on doing them. Be like Jesus. Live in the spirit.'

Some people may object that this puts too much emphasis upon our own good deeds. They say we should instead relax and appreciate the free gift of God's love and mercy. There is value in this objection. Surely it expresses a strong emphasis in the Bible. But just as strong is the emphasis on the everyday outworking, in the individual and corporate life of Christians, of Jesus' way of love. Our worship will reflect how we balance these two mutually supporting emphases: God's free grace and our obedient response.

LET US WALK AS CHILDREN OF LIGHT

Reader A: Let us walk as children of light!

ALL: WE BELONG TO CHRIST. WE ARE CLOTHED WITH THE LIFE OF CHRIST HIMSELF.

Reader B: And so there is no difference between us – rich and poor, men and women, black and white, young and old. We are all one in Christ Jesus (Gal. 3.27–8)!

A: If one of us suffers, we all suffer together. If one member is honoured, we all celebrate together. May there be no discord among us, because we all care for one another (I Cor. 12.25).

B: Let us not be negligent about meeting together. But rather let us encourage each other and consider how to stir one another up to love and good works (Heb. 10.24–5).

A: If our love is genuine, we will outdo one another in showing honour. We will contribute to each other's needs and practice generous hospitality (Romans 12.10, 13).

B: We will reject the craving and love of money, which is the root of all evil. May we learn to be content, and to share in simplicity of heart (I Tim. 6.8).

ALL: IT IS LOVE, THEN, THAT IS OUR AIM. LOVE BINDS EVERYTHING TOGETHER IN PERFECT HARMONY (I Cor. 14.1; Col. 3.5).

A: If we walk in the light as God is in the light, we have fellowship with one another. And the blood of Jesus his Son cleanses us from all sin. (I John 1.7).

ALL: LET US WALK AS CHILDREN OF LIGHT!

The biblical themes in this reading are positive ones: stressing economic sharing, treating one another with honour, showing generous hospitality, living in contentment. And these are presented, not as scolding in areas in which we have failed yet again, but as encouragement to the whole church. This vision of the Church inspires us as we pray. We are children of God, cleansed by Jesus' blood and marked with his humility.

Confessing together his love and our commitment to him, we are walking in his light.

By using two readers and ALL, we emphasise the corporate nature of the prayer. The whole church prays together using 'we' and 'us.' The effect of this is very different from a confession stressing individual moral failures followed by a statement of absolution.

Jesus' Prayer For His Disciples

A shorter meditation is based on Jesus' prayer in John chapter 17 for his disciples – for us. How beneficial it is for us to hear and repeat over and again Jesus' own deepest concern – that his disciples might have unity among themselves. Jesus knew so well that dissension works devastation on even the most eloquent verbal witness to the Father's saving love for the world.

In this reading the leader needs to pace this meditation properly, allowing an appropriate pause between each of the five sections.

JESUS' PRAYER FOR HIS DISCIPLES

Leader: Jesus prayed. Holy Father, keep those you have given me true to your name.

ALL: LORD JESUS, ARE OUR INTENTIONS, OUR ACTIONS, TRUE TO YOUR NAME? LORD, MAKE US TRUE. (pause)

Leader: May they be one, Father, as we are one.

ALL: LORD, ARE WE REALLY ONE IN YOUR SPIRIT? HEAL OUR DIVISIONS. SHOW US HOW TO BE TRUTHFUL. (pause)

Leader: Father, the world hates them because they do not belong to the world.

ALL: LORD, ARE WE CONFRONTING THE WORLD'S VALUES, ITS SEDUCTIONS? GIVE US COURAGE. KEEP OUR EYES FIXED ON YOU. WE BELONG TO YOU, NOT TO THE WORLD. (pause)

Leader: Make them holy, Father, in the truth. Your word is truth.

ALL: LORD JESUS, YOU ARE THE WAY, THE TRUTH, THE LIFE. (pause)

Leader: May they be so completely one that the world will realise that it is you who has sent me. May the world realise that I have loved them as much as you have loved me.

ALL: LORD GOD, REMIND US EVERY DAY THAT YOU SENT YOUR SON NOT TO CONDEMN THE WORLD, BUT THAT THROUGH HIM THE WORLD MIGHT BE SAVED.

The reading above creates the effect of our listening to Jesus praying. Sentence by sentence, we reflect upon each petition. The natural response is to examine our lives, and to resolve to adhere to Jesus' desire for us.

That You May Have Life

Based on Matthew chapter 5, the following reflective confession allows Jesus' words to remind us of God's promise of life and joy. But at the same time it calls us into the realities of everyday life in which we are discovering the presence of God's reign.

Its source is the most vital and refreshing one for corporate prayers of confession and new resolution – the Beatitudes. Not only do these statements succinctly sum up Jesus' life and teaching, they remind us that the one who spoke and lived these words is the one who lives among us now and makes it possible to walk in his steps. Jesus enables us to follow him on the narrow way.

THAT YOU MAY HAVE LIFE

Leader: Do we have ears to hear? Then let us listen. Jesus says:

Jesus (J): I have come that you may have life, and that you may have it in fullness. But the gate is narrow and the way is not easy that leads to life. And so, enter in by the narrow gate. Come, follow me. (pause)

J: Follow me in understanding true poverty of spirit.

Reader (R):   God, help us. Show us our poverty, strip us of our greed and our false security in the riches of this world. Let us value only the security of your care, the treasures of your kingdom.

J: When you place yourselves with the poor people of this world, the kingdom of God is among you. (pause)

J;   Come, follow me. Follow me as I show you how to mourn.

R: God, help us. Soften our hardened hearts. Give us hearts of compassion for the pain of our world, for the pain of our neighbours, of our Christian sisters and brothers, and for the pain of our enemies.

J: When you mourn, when you grieve over the world as I do, you will be comforted. (pause)

J: Come, follow me. Follow me into true meekness.

R: God, help us. Make us gentle. Root out our selfish and wilful ways. Teach us patience and endurance. Help us to receive your gifts without the price of our striving, without our efforts.

J: When you become truly meek you will inherit the earth. (pause)

J: Come, follow me. Follow me into a passion for justice.

R: God, help us. Forgive our complacency. Give us an insatiable desire to see your justice, your reign coming in our lives, in our churches, in our world.

J: When you hunger and thirst for God and his justice, you will be satisfied. (pause)

J: Come, follow me. Follow me into purity of heart.

R: God, help us. Open up a pure source of life within. Help us to go beyond a measured doing of good deeds. Lead us into a life of freedom in your Spirit. Lord, make our hearts your home.

J;   When you seek for purity of heart, you will see God.

J: You are already made clean by the word which I have spoken to you. Abide in me. As the branch cannot bear fruit by itself, unless it abides in the vine, neither can you, unless you abide in me. I am the vine, you are the branches. If you abide in me you will bear much fruit, but apart from me you can do nothing. I have spoken these things to you so that my joy may be in you. So that your joy may be full.

One of the benefits of using Jesus' words like this is that we are able to linger a few minutes on each idea. The Beatitudes are distilled wisdom, more poetic than mere instruction or description. Reading the passage straight through can give only a superficial effect. In this reading the altered grammatical point of view allows Jesus to address us directly. We are able to meditate briefly on each idea, and then we pray for ourselves in light of Jesus' words to us.

E: Inter-Weaving Scripture for Confession

Surprising insights appear when Old and New Testament passages are placed side by side. In the prayers that follow, I have interwoven verses from psalms, gospels and letters. Composite prayers from sources spanning centuries of human experience dramatise that God is consistent throughout time, culture and geography. The one whom Jesus called Abba is the God whom the psalmists called Yahweh. And he is the one who reaches out to us in mercy and healing.

WALK IN THE WAY JESUS WALKED

Reader A: If we walk in the light as God is in the light, we have fellowship with one another, and the blood of Jesus, God's son, cleanses us from sin. If we say we have no sin, we deceive ourselves and the truth is not in us.

Reader B: Lord, at last I admitted to you I had sinned, no longer concealing my guilt. I said, I will go to the Lord and confess my fault. And you, you have forgiven the wrong I did, and have pardoned my sin.

A: If we confess our sins, he is faithful and just, and will forgive us our sins and cleanse us from all unrighteousness.

B: Happy is the one whose fault is forgiven, whose sin is blotted out. Happy is the one whom the Lord accuses of no guilt, whose spirit is purified of deceit.

A: My little children, I am writing this to you so that you may not sin. But if anyone does sin, we have an advocate with the Father, Jesus Christ, the righteous. By this we may be sure that we know him, if we keep his commandments.

B: Whosoever keeps God's word, in him truly love for God is made perfect. By this we may be sure that we are in him: if we abide in God we will walk in the same way that Jesus walked (I John, Psalm 32).

In the preceding reading the grammatical point of view has remained unaltered. The psalm is in the first person singular and the New Testament verses are in first person plural. This difference unites individual and corporate confession.

SEEK ME WHILE I MAY BE FOUND

This reading is similar to the one preceding, but draws on a wider range of Scripture.

Reader A: The Lord says: Seek me while I may be found. Call upon me while I am near. Leave behind your wicked ways. Stop thinking in unjust ways. Return to me, and I will have mercy on you. Come back to me, for I will generously give you pardon (Isa. 55.6–7).

Reader B: If we say we have no sin, we deceive ourselves, and the truth is not in us (I John 1.8).

140

Reader A: Have mercy on us, O God, and put a new and right spirit within us. Cast us not away from your presence, and take not your Holy Spirit from us. Restore to us the joy of your salvation, and uphold us with a willing spirit (Ps. 51.6–9).

B: If we confess our sins, he is faithful and just and will forgive us our sins and cleanse us from all unrighteousness (1 John 1.9).

A: We will trust in the steadfast love of God for ever and ever. We will thank you forever for what you have done! We will proclaim your name, for it is good, in the presence of the whole world (Ps. 52.8–9)!

B: If we walk in the light as he is in the light, we have fellowship with one another, and the blood of Jesus, his Son, cleanses us from sin (I John 1.7).

A: If we say we have no sin, we deceive ourselves and the truth is not in us. (I John 1.8)

B: Lord, at last I admitted to you I had sinned, no longer concealing my guilt. I said, I will go to the Lord and confess my fault.

A: And you, you have forgiven the wrong I did and have pardoned my sin.

B: Happy is the one whose fault is forgiven, whose sin is blotted out. Happy is the one whom the Lord accuses of no guilt, whose spirit is purified of deceit (Ps. 32.1).

A: My little children, I am writing this to you so that you may not sin. But if anyone does sin, we have an advocate with the Father, Jesus Christ the righteous.

B: By this we may be sure that we know him, if we keep his commandments.

A: Whoever keeps God's word, in that person love for God is truly perfected.

B: By this we may be sure that we are in him. If we say we abide in God, we will walk in the same way Jesus walked (I John 2.6).

This reading takes a few ideas from two New Testament letters and places them side by side. In their original contexts the ideas are part of dense and extended theological passages. By breaking the reading into small segments for different voices and choosing an appropriate reading pace, the words, though familiar, assume fresh perspective.

Reader A: Now this is the message that we have heard from God's Son, and announce to you: God is light and there is no darkness at all in him. If we then say that we have fellowship with him, yet at the same time we live in the darkness, we are lying both in our words and in our actions.

Reader B: If we say that we have no sin, we deceive ourselves and there is no truth in us (I John 18).

(silence)

A: Now God's way of putting people right with himself has been revealed. God puts people right through their faith in Jesus Christ. God does this for all who believe in Jesus Christ because there is no difference at all:

B: Everyone has sinned and is far away from God's saving presence.

A: But by the free gift of God's grace all are put right with him through Jesus Christ, who sets us free (Romans 3).

B: If we live in the light as he is in the light, then we have fellowship with one another, and the blood of Jesus purifies us from every sin (I John 1.7).

A: There is no condemnation now for those who live in union with Christ Jesus. For the law of the Spirit, which brings us life in union with Christ Jesus, has set us free from the law of sin and death.

B: The spirit that God has given us does not make us slaves or cause us to be afraid. Instead, the Spirit makes us God's children, and by the spirit's power we cry out to God: Father, Abba, Father. God's Spirit joins himself to our spirits to declare that we are God's children (Romans 8.1,15–16).

LORD, HEAR OUR PRAYER!

This reading juxtaposes parts of a psalm with parts of an epistle. The intense desire of the psalmist for God's presence is interwoven with the near despair of Paul as he contemplates the tensions between good and evil within him. The second part of the reading exults in God's grace and love, combining perspectives which are centuries apart. The reading closes with a plea for God's presence on the continuing way through life.

Reader A: Lord, hear our prayer! In your righteousness listen to our pleas. Answer us in your faithfulness (Ps. 143).

Reader B: I know that good does not live in me – that is, in my human nature. For even though the desire to do good is in me, I am not able to do it. I don't do the good that I want to do. Instead I do the evil that I don't want to do. I know that good does not live in me. (pause)

Reader B continues: My heart, my inner being, delights in the law of God. But I see a different law at work in my body. O, how unhappy I am! Who will rescue me from this body that is taking me to death? (Romans 7.18,24).

A: I wait eagerly for the Lord's help, and in his word I trust. I wait for the Lord more eagerly than watchmen wait for the dawn – than watchmen wait for the dawn (Ps. 130.5–6). (pause)

B: God's way of putting people right with himself has now been revealed. It has nothing to do with the law, even though the law of Moses and the prophets gave their witness to it. God puts people right through their

143

faith in Jesus Christ. God does this for all who believe
in Christ because there is no difference at all: everyone
has sinned and is far away from God's presence. But by
the free gift of God's grace all are put right with him
through Christ Jesus, who sets them free (Romans
3.21–24).

A: Thanks be to God, who does this through our
Lord Jesus Christ!

B: Remind me each morning of your constant love,
for I put my trust in you. My prayers go up to you; show
me the way I should go (Ps. 143.8).

A: You are our God. Teach us to do your will. Be
good to us, and guide us on a safe path (Ps. 143.10).

B: With you, Lord, is the spring of life. In your light
we see light. Lord, extend your mercy to all who turn to
you (Ps. 36.9).

Leader: Lord God, grant your people grace to
withstand temptation, so that with pure hearts and
minds we may follow you, the only God, through Jesus
Christ our Lord. Amen.

F. Inter-Weaving Hymn Verses and Bible Passages

Carefully prepared readings can be woven into periods
of 'free' worship, and can provide seed for the Spirit to
enrich our expressions of response to God. There is no
richer source of nourishment for our corporate worship
than the words of Scripture – the words of Jesus, the
words of the prophets, the words of the psalmists and
letter-writers, the visionaries and the poets.

Scripture can speak with special freshness through
our prayers of confession when we place the words of
our hymns and songs next to Bible verses. Light can
shine in both directions, and the meanings in both
sources can be intensified. For example, after a reading
of a Scripture passage, the congregation can sing the
verse of the hymn; or someone can *read* the hymn
verse, thereby casting new emphasis on familiar words.

By reading the hymn verses, we allow a literary form – the poem – to stand alone in worship. This will probably provoke objection from some people. Resistance to art forms in worship (music, dance, visual elements) has a long history among Christians. Resistance to poetry reading in particular may be stronger in Western and European churches than in churches of other countries where poetry is a people's art form. In Eastern Europe or in Africa, crowds will sit and listen with absorption to poems both old and new. Those of us who resist using poems in worship should gently remind ourselves that if poetry in the Bible is so precious, then poetry written by Christians out of their experience and involvement has value, too. Such poetry should find its proper place in our public worship.

Variety in the pitch of speaking voices, as well as care in inflection and emphasis, can enliven these readings. It is essential to begin reading only when everyone is fully ready and expectant, especially if the reading is short. The reader will know when to start by looking directly into the eyes of the people.

The three following examples of interwoven hymn texts and Scripture verses show one way of incorporating poetry into worship. It is not important that the hymn texts in the following examples may not be familiar. They stand here simply as models of a technique of combining Scripture and Christian poetry which is useful and infinitely adaptable.

Example One

If Christ lives in us, the Spirit is life for us because we have been put right with God (Romans 8.10).

> Thou true vine, that heals the nations,
> Tree of life, thy branches we.
> They who leave thee fade and wither,
> None bear fruit except in thee.

Cleanse us, make us sane and simple,
Till we merge our lives in thine,
Gain ourselves in thee, the Vintage,
Give ourselves through thee, the Vine.

Nothing can we do without thee;
On thy life depends each one;
If we keep thy words and love thee,
All we ask for shall be done.

May we, loving one another,
Radiant in thy light abide;
So through us, made fruitful by thee,
Shall our God be glorified.

'TSN' in Songs of Praise, 1925

Example Two

Be merciful to us, O God, because of your constant
love.
Because of your great mercies wipe away our sins.
Wash us from all our evil, and make us clean from our
sins.

(Ps. 51.1–2)

Lord Jesus, I long to be perfectly whole.
I want you forever to live in my soul.
Break down every idol, cast out every fear.
Now wash me and I will be whiter than snow.
Whiter than snow, yes, whiter than snow.
Now wash me and I will be whiter than snow.

James Nicholson, 1872

Create pure hearts within us, O God,
and put a new and right spirit among us.
Do not banish us from your presence,
do not take your Holy Spirit away from us.

Give us again the joy that comes from your salvation
and make us willing to obey you.

(Ps 51.10–2)

Example Three

Reader A: The Lord says:
Heaven is my throne; the earth is my footstool.
All of creation is the work of my hand.
All things are mine.
But this is the one to whom I will look
the one who is humble and contrite in spirit,
the one who trembles at my word.

(Isa. 66.1–2)

Reader B: Lord God, my fault I have laid before you.
I did not hide my sins. I said, I will go to the Lord and
confess my fault. Lord, you have absolved me, forgiving my sins (Ps. 32.5).

Reader C: Father, each child of yours invokes you in
the hour of distress. Should the great rivers overflow,
they cannot reach me. You are a refuge for me. You
keep me from distress (Ps. 32.6).

Open the wells of grace and salvation,
pour the rich streams deep into my heart.
Cleanse and refine my thought and affection,
seal me and make me pure as thou art.

Elisha A. Hoffman, *c.* 1902

For Thought and Action

How is corporate confession different from personal
confession? How is it similar?

Find prayers of confession in historical writers: Augustine, mystics, reformers, poets, etc.

Look up the Prayer of Manasseh, an Old Testament apocryphal book and compare it to biblical confessions.

Outline a prayer of corporate confession, beginning with thanksgiving for God's actions in your church's story, reflecting on hard-heartedness and disobedience, moving into receiving God's word of healing, and making a commitment to corporate life modelled on Jesus.

Does your church emphasise a contradiction between good works and God's grace? Write confession/repentance prayers for your church which incorporate Scriptures that deal with this tension.

Find Old and New Testament passages that interact in their insights to the heart of God. Prepare confession prayers which highlight these interactions.

Use hymn texts, poems and Scriptures to develop imaginative meditations which include: awareness of God, of ourselves, the will to change, the presence of Jesus in that change.

6: Intercession

Intercession is a word in our passive vocabulary, not our active vocabulary. It isn't an everyday conversational word, although we recognise it, and know what it's about. It sounds formal and churchy. It isn't a 'useful' word. But in fact intercession is the name for something familiar and natural. Intercession is simply an act of pleading one person's cause with another person. The verb 'to intercede' literally means 'to go between'. When we intercede with God on behalf of someone we perform a caring act in which we 'love our neighbours as we love ourselves'.

Intercession is the oxygen prayer for the church. We breathe in a draught of the fresh air of God's care for us and for his world. We breathe out a sigh of empathy and concern for those around us.

A. Doing It Together

This section is about how the congregation prays for itself and for other churches, for the world around us and all of creation. It is about corporate prayer. Many books and seminars help us to learn about private prayer. They answer our questions about how often we should pray, how to be quiet, how to sit or kneel, how to meditate, how to listen to God, how to argue with God and how to pray for others. But here we will think about our praying together – the prayers of our churches – not simply the prayers of individuals alone in their times of private devotion.

Why Pray Together?

Have you ever walked through a corridor of a music conservatory? Behind each door may be a master musician working with a student, listening, correcting, coaching and encouraging. The student learns to breathe well, train his fingers and imagine a beautiful musical phrase. Master and student may be working on one musical line from a large, concerted composition, and together they may achieve a line of beauty.

But that one line finds its destined place within the large musical composition. When many individual musicians come together with their own lines prepared, they join together in trios, chamber orchestras or operatic productions. And what beautiful music can pour out, far beyond the beauty of any one part.

This musical example has a parallel with Christian prayer. As individual Christians pray alone they discipline their minds, give free range to their creative imaginations and learn to listen with patient silence for God's voice. These are significant contributions to corporate prayer. When Christians pray corporately, the inspiration and overview gained in the larger group flows onward into their individual prayer. The converse is also true. Just as a group performance may change the way an individual plays, so corporate prayers may affect an individual's private devotion. When musicians/Christians play/pray together, something powerful and beautiful can happen.

Loving your Neighbour

Church noticeboards list the week's spectrum of activities. Children's groups, women's groups, aid projects, evangelistic or peace activities, bazaars, and friendship groups jostle to fill up the week's free times. Prayer groups are often listed among all the other projects and activities. But in fact, prayer *is* the Church's work. Intercessory prayer is not something to be relegated to a two-hour activity by a few members on one evening of the week (and, parenthetically, inserted into the public worship for a few minutes in Sunday services). Intercessory prayer is too big for a parenthesis!

'What is the greatest commandment?' Jesus was asked one day. He answered, 'Love God, and love your neighbour as yourself ' (Matt. 19.19). This teaching from Jesus is the basis for all aspects of our life, not least the basis for our corporate prayers. Jesus showed us in his own life how to love God and neighbour. To listen to God, to observe our neighbour with compassionate eyes, to care for the neighbour with the appropriate word, touch or prayer – these are the ways Jesus calls us to follow him.

It is beautiful to see that the prayers of early Christians conformed to Jesus' own principle (of combining love for God, neighbour and self) and to his example (of loving people by praying for them). We can look to our Jewish and Roman brothers and sisters of the first and second centuries for a signpost, a model of a biblical way to pray.

B.   Bible Principles in Intercession

Sometimes we forget that the earliest Christians were Jews. In the Roman catacombs we can see wall paintings of Christians standing in prayer postures exactly like those of the Jews. They raised their faces and arms, turning the palms open and upward. Their Jewish habits of prayer had been passed down for centuries. These Jewish insights and habits formed the framework for the prayer of Jesus and his disciples. If we look closely at prayers in both Testaments we can find certain features that are constant. First there is a recounting of what God has done, then petitions and finally the purpose of it all. Let's look at two examples, one from each Testament.

In Solomon's prayer at the dedication of the temple

151

(I Kgs. 8.56–60) he first thanks God for being faithful. 'Not one word has failed of all the good promises through his servant Moses!' Next he makes several petitions: May God continue to be with the people, may God 'turn their hearts to him, to walk in all his ways', and may God 'uphold the cause of his people according to each day's need.' Solomon gives the purpose in his conclusion: 'So that all the peoples of the earth may know that the Lord is God and that there is no other.'

Our New Testament example comes from Paul's letter to Timothy (I Tim. 2.1–7). Nine hundred years after Solomon, Paul wrote down a prayer similar in structure to the one recorded in I Kings. For Paul, thanksgiving is the only climate proper for petitions. In this example Paul links supplication with thanksgiving, urging that 'requests, prayers, intercession and thanksgiving be made for everyone – for kings and all those in authority.' Why? Just as in Solomon's prayer, the purpose is that God's reign over all his creation may be brought to fulfilment: 'This is good and pleases God our Saviour who wants all to be saved and to come to a knowledge of the truth.'

In both of these examples we see that the foundation of petitionary prayers is thanksgiving. And thanksgiving is rooted in remembering. The discipline of grateful memory is as important to a Christian as many hours of patient practising are to a violinist. The old hymn has it right: 'Count your blessings; name them one by one. Count your many blessings; see what God has done.'

God has been loving and faithful, and he is worthy of praise. Specific requests follow, beginning with needs of individuals and the Church as a whole. The prayers then spread outward to encompass concerns for peace and the general good of society.

It is important to pray specifically about our concerns, and yet not tread on people's dignity in public intercessions. I have felt equally uncomfortable with prayers that sound like news bulletins to God of world economic crises, and ones which include too-personal or trivial details of minor ailments. There are more appropriate moments to announce an engagement or to reveal the latest on someone's medical condition. But an intercessory prayer can easily include the acknowledgment that everyone present has specific, personal concerns, many of which we aren't free to mention publicly. A prayer for God's healing peace (shalom) is always appropriate within the intercessions.

Christians are commissioned to exercise the responsible ministry of prayer for those in authority. The conclusion of the prayers is always a lifting of the eyes to see God as King and to glimpse his big vision for his world. God's reign means vastly more than we can imagine, but we are to register our awareness and longing to see God's reign coming in its completeness.

C. Kingdom Prayers

The Bible tells us that when we start to pray, we should begin by thanking God for who he is and what he has done. In the preceding section we noted the importance of disciplined remembering as the foundation for prayer. We need to recall cosmic and historic evidence of God's work – his creation, and his liberation through the Exodus, the Messiah Jesus, and the Holy Spirit. But we also need to be alert to what God is doing now, in our own particular situation.

First the Bad News
Do we believe that God *is* at work in our situations? Sometimes we see so little evidence that he is doing anything about the painful conflicts and dilemmas of our workmates and neighbours. Bad news at work, bad news in the papers, bad news on the telly – everywhere, it's just bad news! What a relief it would be to go to church and shut it all out, even for a short while. After

all, the Bible tells us to put aside all the corruption and malice of the world, and think about things that are lovely and pure (Phil. 4.8).

But God's kingdom coming and his will being done means that, on every front, the good news is confronting the bad news. However small the malice, however petty the corruption, God wants to overcome the evil with good. Often tempted to despair, we should instead practice the disciplined hope Paul described in Romans 8.20–5. All of creation longs for God's liberation, and we participate in that longing with patient but expectant hope. Sometimes we blame God for doing nothing to correct or punish evil, but at the same time we neglect our own job in the battle.

In this battle Christians aren't war correspondents. Taking risks with everyone else, we are actively involved. We make connections. We give encouragement. We go where we are sent. We are messengers, not just journalists.

But our job is not *simply* being messengers. We are called both to imaginative empathy, and to action on behalf of those caught up in the pain and evil of the world. 'Remember those in prison, as if you were their fellow prisoners, and those who are mistreated, as if you yourselves were suffering' (Heb. 13.3).

Throughout the Bible the word 'remember' is a signpost to worship. We remember God's actions and goodness; we remember the plight of the suffering. And in our prayers we bring the two together. We don't filter out the bad news. In our kingdom prayers the good news confronts the bad news. God cares! God is active!

And then the Good News
Jesus told his followers that 'the Kingdom of God is among you' (Luke 17.21). If this is true, it is great news! Let's uncover the evidence. Let's take the time to see what is actually happening around us. If we look for

God expectantly, we will find him here, active now.

Looking for God's actions in the world around us is like going out into the garden to see the first shoots pushing through the ground. Our intercession time can start out with 'reports from the scouts'. We can hear what people have observed around them during the week: A family has found housing, a widow has been comforted, new neighbours have been welcomed and prayers for healing have been answered. 'God is here!' someone suddenly calls out. The shoots of God's reign are pushing through the soil.

Now our prayers of intercession can take their rightful place as nourishers, waterers and groomers. Our prayers can encourage the growth of those unmistakable signs of the kingdom. But it all sounds so ordinary, so uneloquent, so unliturgical. If we let our public prayers become too 'ordinary', how can we determine a line between 'specific' (a good thing) and 'inappropriately personal' (not a good thing)? Are these practical observations and everyday prayers too mundane for public Sunday worship?

Probably not. Our prayers and our worship reflect our understanding of who God is. If we insist upon emphasising God's remoteness and severe perfection, our prayers will be severe and remote. But if we see the God of the Bible as one who lovingly nurtures his children and cares about right relationships, then our prayers will mirror those qualities. Our prayers will demonstrate our understanding of God as the one who cares passionately about justice and is working to bring about joy, freedom and healing.

Joy and freedom and healing sound great. But how do we get there from here? Do we have a part in getting our world there? How do we know what is God's will 'on earth as in heaven' (Matt. 6.10)? How do we know what to pray?

Praying what we Know to be God's Will

The Bible in one hand, and the newspaper in the other!
Richard Foster, in *Celebration of Discipline,* describes
a faithful Christian at prayer. 'We have a spiritual
obligation to penetrate the inner meaning of events and
political pressures, not to gain power, but to gain
prophetic perspective.'[21] As we meditate on the evil
effects of pride and selfish power, we can listen for
God's word to us about them. We can search the
Scriptures and we can pray wordless, listening prayers
in order to gain God's perspective.

Once we have done all that, we can put words into
prayer. The Spirit is with us to show truth, and guide us
in our prayers, even praying for us when we can't
express ourselves. Jesus gave us words that we can pray
with confidence: 'Your kingdom come, your will be
done, on earth as it is in heaven' (Matt. 6.10).

D.   Symbols for Kingdom Prayers

The events, conversations and instinctive knowledge
that God is present in our everyday life are signs of the
kingdom. Can we dramatise or symbolise this reality in
our corporate prayer?

A very simple object can be a symbol. When on a
recent visit to Belfast I heard about a child's handkerchief tied to an iron fence. Meaningless to an outsider,
that tiny piece of cloth held great symbolic power for
local people. Every time they pass by, they remember
two dead children, struck in a disastrous car chase. The
fluttering handkerchief reminds ordinary folk of their
powerlessness. They are caught in political and historical
forces beyond their understanding, and certainly
beyond their choice. That handkerchief is a visual
poem. It hints at meanings much bigger than itself.

We Christians know the symbolic power of water. It
has many associations throughout Scripture, in its
essential contributions to our own everyday lives, and in
the Church's rite of baptism.

All Christians know, too, the power of dramatic symbol in our re-enactment of Jesus' meal with his disciples in the upper room. We discipline and aid our memory by repeating the actions of that unforgettable night. The bread and wine of the meal demonstrate a quality of symbolic power, similar to that of the handkerchief tied to the iron fence. An ordinary, everyday object can point to more profound meanings.

The cross is also a potent symbol. In Western Christianity it has been a sign of 'guilt and shame.' But for many centuries to Christians in Ethiopia the cross has been a symbol of radiating power. In one textile rendering of the cross, each of the four shafts has three sprouts, representing apostles, pushing out at the ends. Twelve good news-bringers invade the surrounding space of darkness with light and freedom!

We encounter symbols every single day of our lives, as we go to work or to the shops. Advertisers are skilled at manipulating us through the hidden power of symbols; sometimes we feel powerless to resist. We could rephrase Luther's indignant comment when some people objected to his setting religious words to secular music: 'Why should the devil have all the good tunes?' Indeed, why should the world around us be so adept in the use of symbols, and we so clumsy? Literal words can't say it all!

Themes and Symbols
'Neighbours' was a theme for our prayers on a recent Sunday. One person told of an incident involving new neighbours moving in next door; another told of conflict over a noisy party; a third recounted friendship between little children in the street. Then we defined 'neighbours' more broadly, and the prayers broadened to include our city, the nation and the world. Lighting a candle for each intercession focused the prayers.

Here's another theme – international food supply patterns – and how our church organised intercessions during One World Week. Sacks full of rice, maize meal, and dried beans sat on the centre table. Beside them were dishes of raisins, hazel nuts, dried apricots and sesame seeds. We talked about the food, pointed on a map to the countries where it came from and described who eats it every day. Prayers centred around thanks for God's provision of food, the need for care of the earth, fair trading practices, relief efforts among starving people and greater sharing of our world's resources.

A world map, photos, posters or large cartoons in full view on the walls of the church can help the prayer times. They also remind people to pray as they come and go. Visitors to a church building can tell a great deal about the concerns of that congregation by the pictures and posters in the entrance. The range of our prayers is part of our witness.

In a larger congregation, people can be given a minute to write concerns for intercession on slips of paper. Later on, during the communion service, baskets with the prayer slips rest beside the bread and wine on the table – tangible symbols of the church's concern for and commitment to the needs of the world.

White roses, red roses, a broken length of a prisoner's chain, white poppies, a photo of crossed warheads, a UB-40 form, a teacup and saucer, a lump of yeast, a mortar and pestle – any of these, laid on the table beside the cup and the bread re-inforce those central symbols of our faith. Each object, a tangible poem, points us to interconnections with the mystery of Jesus' life, death, and new life in the world. Pentecost Sunday in our church is the day for everyone to wear red – the colours of fire and light are powerful.

Christians in many cultures have gone ahead of us Western Europeans in the process of using symbols to help in their worship. Charles Elliott, in *Praying the Kingdom*, gives a number of examples from Ashanti, Sri Lankan, and Indian churches where the local 'language' of visual symbols communicates the Gospel in non-verbal eloquence.[22]

However we go about it, when we Christians intercede together, mysterious things can happen. Irina Ratushinskaya, the Russian Christian poet, describes her last days in solitary confinement in the Mordovian labour camp:

> On the eleventh day [of solitary confinement] . . . I lie on the floor. The hand under my head has been numb for a long time, and I do not feel either the knotty floorboards or the draught from the window. I have no more debts to anyone: they have been paid, and the books balanced. A strange warmth steals over what is left of my body.
>
> I did not know, then, that on that very day a service of intercession was being held for me in a far-off English city, that Soviet diplomats everywhere were being pressured about my case, that a new commandant, Zuykov, would arrive tomorrow . . . [The next day Zuykov said] 'We can no longer hold you here. Get your things, and we'll take you home.'[23]

Sometimes we forget that we ourselves, Christians gathered in worship, are a symbol to the watching world. Christians praying, hearts linked across national barriers, can touch a place of immense longing and hope in people searching for evidence of God's love in our divided world.

Unity
Jesus prayed, 'May they all be one . . . so that the world may believe' (John 17.21). We must join what Jesus joined – his love for the world and the potential witness of his followers' unity of spirit. Can we find symbols that will fuel our desire for unity and solidarity with the trans-national body of Christ?

Symbols that will turn our stomachs over the deprivation and oppression of brothers and sisters in Christ? Symbols which would stimulate those sensitive muscles, the ones that direct a pen across a cheque made out to an aid agency? Symbols that will draw us to pray more passionately for the condition of the unemployed, destitute and weak who also name the name of Christ?

Jesus' simple prayer distils the question of unity. For us it is so complicated and difficult that we too easily give up our efforts. But Jesus doesn't let us squirm out of prayer and action toward unity. Peace and unity, all too elusive, among Christians should be a consistent basis for work towards unity among all peoples.

And so as we prepare for our corporate prayers, let's not shrink from a bold dream of peace among peoples. Let's expand our imaginative capacities in praying for justice among conflicting groups and for freedom for political prisoners. Our prayers will then be in tune with the one Jesus taught us: 'Your kingdom come, your will be done on earth as in heaven.'

E. Who Do We Pray For?

In the early chapters of Acts, Luke gives us a vivid picture of the internal life of the earliest Christians during the weeks and months after Pentecost. He says, 'They devoted themselves to the apostles' teaching and fellowship, to the breaking of bread, and the prayers' (Acts 2.42).

These communal acts were the foundation of their worship, and were the basis of the effective spread of the Gospel among neighbours and inquirers. The epistles show the strong intercession which undergirds the missionary work of the church. '. . . my heart's desire and prayer to God for them is that they may be saved' (Romans 10.1).

Jesus had prayed powerfully for his disciples and his prayer for the safety and unity of his followers was continued among the early Christians. The New Testament epistles are full of requests for prayer and pledges of support from one small church to another.

One of the beauties of praying for each other in the church is that this act brings us closer to the unity that Jesus desired. It is hard to remain judgmental of a person or group for whom we are praying. Honest prayer for someone we despise or accuse often reveals a greater truth to us. We see ourselves and the others both needing God's mercy. A unity in compassion can grow out of the unity in our need for grace. Jesus explained this to us over and again – we experience forgiveness in the measure that we are willing to extend forgiveness.

Praying for the Enemy

'Bless those who curse you. Pray for those who abuse you' (Luke 6.28). Jesus can't be serious! How can we pray for those who malign our friends, who torture and imprison Christians, who dismiss our convictions and ridicule our faith! We feel unable to do anything more than look on in stupefied horror and complain bitterly to each other. Above all, we learn to be practical and keep our own heads down, out of danger.

But Jesus was truly practical and realistic. He knew the heart of his Father, and he had the clear eye of the prophet. Jesus recalled Jeremiah, prophet to sixth-century BC Hebrews. Jeremiah was living in Jerusalem just before the city was burned – and its residents dispersed into captivity – by the national enemy, Babylon. His advice was eloquent, practical and humane. He spoke in the name of the Lord God of Israel, because he understood God's vision of justice and peace among the nations:

161

'Seek the welfare of the city where I have sent you into exile. Pray to the Lord on its behalf, for in its welfare you will find your welfare' (Jer. 29.7).

If we live in a city or nation hostile to God, Christian values and life, we must pray for our city, our rulers. That is the Bible way.

If we live in a country which is open to our free practice of religious life, we need no less to pray for our governors. Our government exists by God's provision. We should 'encourage it to a godly fulfilment of its calling.' As John Gladwin has remarked, the praying church 'can never be indifferent to proper order in society, to the just and proper exercise of power and to the protection of the weak from the abuses of the strong.' Christians are called to prayer for those in political power to keep them from the 'ever-present temptation . . . to use power selfishly and unjustly'.[24]

We live in a world possessed. We see the grip of evil forces over neighbours and ourselves. In the communal violence of such places as Ulster, South Africa or Sri Lanka these forces of evil openly show their frightening grip. But many aspects of our own corporate lives in society are also influenced by evil forces which are unseen or unrecognised.

The effect of Christ's victory over the powers of death is vastly greater than we know or can imagine. In Colossians chapter 2, verse 15, we read that on the cross he 'disarmed the powers and authorities, he made a public spectacle of them, triumphing over them.' We can't comprehend the full meaning of this victory. Yet we sense the truth of the allusion to forces beyond our sight which have great control in our society. Christians require courageous determination to oppose contemporary idolatry. These struggles call on the prayer power of the church.

Scales must fall from our eyes so that we see how to pray for the churches and for others in places of immense conflict. We are not helpless. We are responsible to love our neighbours, our brothers and sisters and our enemies. We combat the powers of darkness with prayer in the name of Jesus the Victor. Intercession is the work of the Church.

F. Bringing Our Prayers to a Close

What was the point of Solomon's prayer? That 'all the peoples of the earth may know that the Lord is God' (I Kgs. 8.60). Similarly, Paul urged his friends to pray to God 'who wants all to be saved and to come to a knowledge of the truth' (I Tim. 2.4). Jesus' prayer was 'that the world may know . . . that you have loved them even as you have loved me' (John 17.23). These three prayers remind us how big is God's vision for humanity.

That vision is, in fact, for all of creation (see Eph. 1.10; Col. 1.20). Our intercessions for ourselves, for the world around us, for our governors, for the natural creation – all point to the transforming vision that carries the whole biblical story along, from Genesis to Revelation. Our prayers should always close with this marvellous sense of the scope of God's kingdom coming, even if we now see it only dimly.

Our intercessions reveal our limited horizons. Petitions often circle around ourselves and are specific to our own immediate concerns. We forget that we are part of a bigger picture, called to solidarity with our brothers and sisters, and responsible for the care of the natural order. Intercession requires discipline for the memory and stimulation for the imagination. An excellent way to exert such discipline and stimulation is through incorporating biblical texts into our prayers.

They shall not hurt or destroy in all my holy
  mountain
for the earth shall be full of the knowledge of God
as the waters cover the sea (Isa. 11.9).

Then will the eyes of the blind be opened
and the ears of the deaf unstopped.
Then will the lame leap like a deer,
and the mute tongue shout for joy.

Water will gush forth in the wilderness
and streams in the desert.
The burning sand will become a pool,
the thirsty ground bubbling springs (Isa. 35.5–7a).

When we go back into the everyday world, we
carry biblical images ingrained and integrated into
our consciousness. So when we see life around us in
contradiction to God's vision for all creation, these
parting images will inspire our day-by-day
responses.

Then he showed me the river of the water of life
bright as crystal
flowing from the throne of God
through the middle of the city.

On either side of the river, the tree of life,
with its twelve kinds of fruit
yielding its fruit each month.

And the leaves of the tree were for
the healing of the nations (Rev. 22.1–2).

Don't these powerful biblical images, rich with
symbols, convey God's vision for the world that
Jesus told us his Father loves so much? Don't they
make our pulses quicken or make tears spring to our
eyes? They touch deep springs inside us, and in their

poetic power they can comfort and inspire us. This vision of God's plan for comprehensive healing is the Bible way to close our prayers of intercession.

For Thought and Action

How is a congregation's prayer affected by the quality of the members' private prayer?

Pray with confidence what we know to be God's will.

Thanksgiving is a foundation for intercession, and disciplined hope builds on thanksgiving. Do we expect to see God at work through the week's events?

Follow the news and observe current events to penetrate their inner meanings. Take seriously the churches' call to prophetic perspective. Build prayer on this foundation.

How do you determine appropriateness of public prayer for private or trivial details? Are various settings for corporate prayer readily available – with one or two others, in special prayer task-groups, in general public worship?

The whole church can pledge specific intercessions during the week ahead as a concrete way to obey Jesus' command: Love your neighbour as yourself.

Write a 'shalom' prayer which could be used regularly in worship. It might be short enough for all to learn and use it throughout the week.

Commission members to find symbols to use in different parts of worship – banners, actions, objects.

Develop themes for prayers – link in to God's kingdom concerns as we 'read' our everyday life.

Checklist for corporate intercessions:
    for the local church life.
    for prisoners.
    for unity among Christians, for other churches.
    for peace.
    for neighbours and others to know God.
    for healing of all kinds.
    for the government.
    for the enemy.
    for the principalities and powers.
    for the care of the earth.

7:   At Table With The Lord

You could see them in a thousand places around the earth – Christians gathered around a table, sharing a meal. They do this to remember a particular meal on a particular evening 2,000 years ago.

English-speaking Christians use a marvellous variety of words for our re-enactment of that meal instituted by Jesus and established by the early Church. We have the Greek word *agape* as well as the Greek-derived Eucharist. We have used a Latin root for communion. Middle English gives us table and from Old French, supper. Paying close attention to which words we use helps us enter more fully into commemorating Jesus' meal with his disciples. Eucharist says 'thank you'; communion 'sharing'; *agape* says 'love'; table and supper remind us of hospitality, sharing and reaching out to include others.

Christians have wonderful religious language but our actions unfortunately have not matched our words. All too often the 'thank you' of Eucharist has been experienced as 'you can only say thank you in these forms, in these clothes, in this building and in this language.' Communion 'sharing' has become 'we only share among ourselves'. The love and hospitality of *agape* have been stymied by pride and loveless attitudes. It's not been a happy history.

Though this is not the place to argue over eucharistic doctrine and Christian unity, we must keep in mind how closely linked the two are. And we need to remember how deeply Jesus desired unity among his followers. He prayed, 'Father, may they all be one'

(John 17.21 RSV). To see his people divided, his own body broken, separated instead of united at his table, pierces his heart. The laziness, ignorance and hardness of heart that keep us apart are all sin. When we separate ourselves, we reject God's loving intention to bring all together in Christ Jesus (Col. 1.20).

Christians should care deeply about the divisions among us. We should pray, change our thoughts and find new ways to work together and to express God's gift of unity. Unity in his name is the quality that Jesus most desired to see among his disciples.

We Christians know that we are shamefully divided. But what can we do about it? Our histories seem to capture us and bind us apart.

A. The Agape Meal

One way that some Christians work towards broader Christian fellowship has been through the 'agape meal'. The modern agape is based on the love feast of the early Church. Both practical and ceremonial, the agape meals for New Testament Christians were central to the churches' life. 'They broke bread in their homes and ate together with glad and sincere hearts' (Acts 2.46). Sometimes these modern efforts to bring Christians together in the agape meal are discounted. 'It's ineffective! It ignores the sad truth of Christian disunity!' say the detractors. 'We must face the facts of our differences!'

Yet the love feast can be a good expression of Christian unity. In the context of remembrance and thanksgiving, we experience hospitality and economic sharing. These themes, powerful in the inner life and outer witness of the earliest Christians, need to be lived out in fresh ways in every generation. The agape meal shared among Christians in their homes or neighbourhood clusters, could become a powerful sign of the kingdom, an expression of unity among Jesus' followers. This meal could also perpetuate Jesus' inclusion of 'sinners' and outsiders. He often shared table fellowship with people on the fringes of society. If Christians followed his example, our agape meals could be practical Good News.

The agape meal appears in the New Testament as the shared supper of the early Christians. The 'breaking of bread' in Acts chapter 2 and the description of the meal in I Corinthians chapter 11, testify to regular table fellowship. This table sharing became problematic because of abuses such as gluttony or drunkenness, but it stands behind two important types of meetings of early Christians. The Eucharist or communion, first observed as a part of an actual meal, eventually was separated from the meal table and formed the closing section of a main worship service of the week. Only bread, wine and water remained as reminders of the origins of the ceremony in an actual meal.

Where and when did the ceremony of bread and wine separate from a real meal? If only we knew. The separation probably came at different times in different geographic regions. Documented evidence of agape meals are available to use from diverse parts of the Roman Empire. Prayers to accompany a Syrian agape meal are found in *The Didache*.[25] In AD 197 Tertullian describes an agape in Carthage in his *Apology*.[26] A full description of an early second-century Roman agape meal appears in a short church manual written by Bishop Hippolytus.[27] But many questions persist. Between the New Testament references to a central Christian meal and descriptions of agape meals at the turn of the second century we lack firm evidence about the separation of Sunday Eucharist from agape meal.

Meanwhile the agape meal, practised in the homes of Christians, continued to express unity and economic redistribution within the Church. It revealed direct links with the fellowship meals of Jesus and his friends.

A Commemoration of the Meal in the Upper Room

Our church first used the following order of service when we set out to learn more about the background to the Last Supper which Jesus ate with his disciples. We found that in Jesus' time it was quite usual for people to form religious dinner clubs, called *chaburah*. This is probably what Jesus' Last Supper appeared to be – a typical chaburah meal. But it was an especially festive one because it was Passover.

This shared Jewish meal was a precursor of the agape meal (love feast) among earliest Christians. Remembrance is always a strong theme in Jewish prayers. Deliverance from bondage, the gift of the Law, the Covenant – all are remembered with thanksgiving to God who so generously and faithfully cared for his people. Notice the manners of hospitality, the service of simplest needs, sharing of food, conversation, prayers and psalm singing.

A chaburah meeting would have been more than a religious and social event. It would have had an economic sharing aspect, too. Giving alms for the poor was an important part of Jewish practice. It is no wonder that when Judas left the upper room before the end of the meal, the disciples at Jesus' table expressed no surprise. They would have assumed he was going out to distribute money for the poor from the group's common fund.

Our church found out quite a bit about the Jewish chaburah supper: the meal involved remembrance, thanksgiving, hospitality and economic sharing. We also discovered that these same themes carried through into the agape meals (love feasts) of the early Christians.

In the following readings for a chaburah meeting, the narrator's part does not need to be obtrusive. It should explain and give the background to what is happening. Simple prayers fill out the commentary and the readings.

A COMMEMORATION OF THE MEAL
IN THE UPPER ROOM

(A young person carries a small bowl with a napkin around to each person present. Each one dips fingertips in the water, then dries on the napkin.)

Host: You are blessed, O Lord our God, eternal King, for you bring forth bread from the earth.

Narrator: Jesus took the bread and broke it as every Jewish householder broke it every evening at every supper table throughout the year. He gave thanks and blessed God as the giver of bread. Then, as he handed the fragments to his disciples, he made the unexpected and mysterious remark:

Host: This is my body which is for you. Do this for the recalling of me.

Prayer I: Lord, you enter our lives in simple ways, through simple things. You put new meaning into the everyday act of eating bread. Teach us what it means to remember you in the sharing of bread. Amen.

(Break and share the bread around the table. Serve the main course of the meal).

N: At the end of the meal, the youngest participant or a servant presented water and a towel again. This was considered a menial task. To everyone's surprise, on this occasion Jesus himself, their Master, took the customary towel and basin. He stooped down and washed, not their hands but their feet. According to Jewish courtesy, in this final washing ceremony the eldest would be served last. And so, last of all, Jesus came to Peter.

Reader I: John 13.6–9, 12–6

N: Then followed the disturbing conversation about someone who would betray Jesus. Judas departed into the night. Some disciples thought he was on an errand, possibly to prepare for the festival or to distribute money to the poor. Jesus said:

Reader II: John 13.31–5

N: At the end of every meal the host recited a long, customary prayer. It was the same in every household. On this festive occasion a special cup of wine, known as 'the cup of blessing', accompanied the typical prayer. At the end of the prayer, the host sipped from the cup, and then passed it to all present.

Host: *(picking up the cup)* Let us give thanks.

All: Blessed be the name of the Lord, from this time forward and for ever more.

Host: With the assent of all present – *(all who assent, nod)* – we will bless him of whose bounty we have partaken.

All: Blessed be the one of whose bounty we have partaken and through whose goodness we live.

Host: Lord, we bless you. You are our God, because you gave us, as a heritage to our fathers, a desirable, good and ample land. We praise you because you brought us up out of the land of Egypt, from the house of bondage. We bless you as well for the Covenant, sealed in our flesh. We thank you for the Law and the Statutes which you have made known to us, and for the life, grace, and loving kindness which you have continually given to us. For all this, O Lord our God, we thank you and bless you. Praised be your Name, by all living creatures, continually and forever.

(Host sips from the cup, then passes it to the others.)

N: As the cup was passed in silence from one person to another, Jesus made a startling remark. It startled because it introduced into the familiar, festive ceremony a new and ambiguously ominous note:

Host: 'This cup is the New Covenant in my blood. Do this whenever you drink it, for the recalling of me.'

Prayer II: Lord, we have blessed you as the God of creation, the sustainer of life. The Jewish people blessed you for the Covenant, sealed in their flesh, which was a sign that they would be your people and you would be their God. We bless you now for the New Covenant, sealed in the blood of Jesus our Lord. Teach us what it means to remember you in the drinking of this cup. Amen.

Singing of a psalm closes the service.

The Agape Meal through the Centuries

For four centuries agape meals were integral to Christian practice. These meals expressed the deep values of the Christian communities in a number of areas, social and economic as well as 'spiritual'.

For these extended Christian families – sometimes called households of faith – agape meals were important social occasions. Gathering around a table with shared food was the most natural of social settings. Though not a religious act, a shared meal became a potent symbol of the new family of God's adopted children. People could be 'brothers and sisters' in a way incredible to members of other social groupings.

In the first few centuries after Jesus, the agape meals served as economic equalisers, and as a means of redistribution in the Christian community. The elder, also called bishop, served not only as liturgical president, but as chief economic officer. The bishop had assistants called deacons. The deacons served as his 'eyes and ears', finding out who was in need and who had things to share.

If a householder wished to hold an agape meal, the bishop would draw up the guest lists. This method assured that the most needy folk were invited to the agape or 'bounty' as it was sometimes called. Some poor folk would get invitations every few days to various households' agape meals. At a meal, admonitions to moderation ensured that leftovers would remain for distribution among poor and widows on the following days. Two Christian virtues joined in agape celebrations: hospitality and economic equalisation.

These meals also included specifically 'spiritual' aspects. Uplifting Scriptures were read out during the meal. The bishop would answer questions and give advice. Hymns and prayers played an important part in the evening's observances.

'How can we who share eternal gifts refuse to share our temporal abundance as well?' the earliest Christians asked themselves.[28] Table hospitality was deeply engrained as essential courtesy among eastern peoples. Christian conscience and gratitude for God's provision combined with typical eastern hospitality to make possible a uniquely integrated celebration. How inspiring that all of these aspects could come together in such an everyday experience as having folks in for a meal!

Here is the earliest surviving description of an agape meal. It is part of a bishops' handbook from third-century Rome. Bishop Hippolytus recounts the events of a typical love feast.

The Agape Meal in Rome (AD 215)
When evening had come, they brought in a lamp. Standing up in the middle of the guests, the bishop (elder) *(lighting the lamp)* gave the greeting:

> The Lord be with you.

And the people replied:

> With your spirit.

The elder said:

Let us give thanks to the Lord.

The people said:

It is fitting and right
Greatness and exaltation with glory are his due.

The elder then prayed:

We give you thanks, Lord, through your Son Jesus Christ our Lord, through whom you have shone upon us and revealed to us the inextiguishable light. So when we have completed the length of the day and have come to the beginning of the night, and have satisfied ourselves with the light of day which you have created for our satisfying; and since now through your grace we do not lack the light of evening, we praise and glorify you through your son our Lord Jesus Christ, through whom be glory and power and honour to you with the Holy Spirit, both now and always and to the ages of ages. Amen.

And all said:

Amen.

The elder blessed the bread, gave thanks, divided and distributed it.

People then ate the meal together with great care for their manners. When they ate and drank they were cautioned to do it 'discreetly and not to the point of drunkenness'. They were not to play the clown, or act in such a way that the host might be 'grieved by disorderly behaviour'. Guests were to pray for their host that he would be worthy to receive his guests, and to pray for God's favour and blessing on him.

Loud talking and arguing were not allowed, but the elder was prepared to answer questions put to him. While the elder spoke, all were to listen and be 'modestly silent'.

Moderation in eating was the rule for these occasions: 'Eat enough for there to be some (left) over'. The host could send the food to others who were hungry. The temperance of his guests ensured that the host could extend his hospitality beyond the circle of guests around his table.

After supper they were to stand and pray. The boys and the young girls said psalms.

The deacon took the cup, reciting one of the Hallel psalms (111–118). Further psalms followed with the people joining in on 'Alleluia' which means: 'We praise him who is God. Glory and praise to him who created every age through his word alone.'

When the psalm recitations were finished, the elder gave thanks over the cup and all the participants shared it among themselves. The end of the meal wasn't the end of the agape. With prayers, thanks and blessings all those leftovers still had to be distributed among the needy.

In summing up, Bishop Hippolytus advised: 'Let everyone eat in the name of the Lord. For this is pleasing to God, that we should compete among the heathen in being of one mind and sober.'[29]

The Agape Meal – Loss and Recovery

For many generations the agape meal formed a vital part of church life, but by the eighth century it had been gradually forgotten. Small groups of Christians throughout the centuries rediscovered and attempted to reinstate it. Pietist groups in Germany and The Netherlands, the Moravians, for example, practised the love feast. In the eighteenth century it was among them that John Wesley observed the love feast and then established it among his societies. Among early Methodists it developed the characteristic of a shared family meal and it was also an occasion for members to testify to their conversions. Once the high point of the Methodist year, the love feast gradually lost its vigour and, regrettably, the practice died out.

One group which found and preserved the agape is the Church of the Brethren, an eighteenth century pietist movement with Anabaptist roots, which is still strong in the United States. For 250 years they have observed the agape in a combined service with foot-washing and Lord's Supper. Their service is an admirable synthesis of practices recorded in Gospel and epistle accounts. Their observance emphasises unity, reconciliation and service, as well as commemorating the Lord's death.

The following describes a love feast held at the home of Johann Gumrie, an eighteenth-century Brethren leader in Pennsylvania.

'They gather around a long table, a hymn is sung and in the silent evening hour, with no witnesses but God, and curious children, these people begin the observance of the ordinances of God's house on Christmas evening, 1723. The sisters on one side, the brethren on the other, arise and wash one another's feet. Then they eat the Lord's Supper, pass the kiss of charity with the right hand of fellowship, partake of the holy communion, sing a hymn and go out.'[30]

In the early days of the Brethren movement the meal was open to visitors. Leftover food was given out to the poor after the meal. It is fascinating to see that originally the Brethren did not neglect this economic aspect of their service as they gleaned details from New Testament practice.

The Simple Church Supper – An Agape Meal?

Here is an idea for a simple church lunch or supper in which Christians from different cultures and traditions could easily participate. The informal home setting is ideal for Christians within a neighbourhood to meet. Everyday hospitality becomes celebratory because it is done 'in the name of Christ'. Instead of having one big carry-in meal for dozens of people in a church hall, people could have little church suppers in local areas and neighbourhoods.

Jesus used simple, common things and made them

special. In his resurrection appearances he took a typical greeting, 'Shalom!' and gave it new significance. He took the everyday bread and wine of the family table and made it deeply significant. Perhaps we, too, could give religious meaning to an ordinary, 'unreligious' carry-in meal.

I know of one church which often organises just such local 'bring and share' meals. Members invite their friends to the meal. Everyone brings something to contribute, however simple it might be. All the food goes on the serving table. After a song and prayer they break and share bread taken from the table before them. People fill their plates and eat the first course of the meal.

At the end of the main course a person designated as host reminds everyone how Jesus shared the meal with his disciples the evening before he died. Then the host gives thanks, holding the cup of wine, and passes it around for all to share. They often pray for each other and for their neighbours and for other concerns. They sing and read another short Scripture passage. The children help to pass out fruit or dessert. Cups of tea accompany the socialising that finishes the time together.

What kind of hybrid Christian observance is this? Is it a eucharist? Yes, it is a thanksgving meal. Is it a communion? Yes, it is a shared meal. Is it table fellowship, hospitality and a pooling of material benefits? Yes, all of those, too. Some would say agape meals create woolly-minded confusion. But is it really confusion? Perhaps celebrating church meals like this more often could serve as a clarification. Maybe the agape meal is a way back to those hallmarks of earliest Christian worship: thanksgiving, remembrance and hospitality.

A Way around, to Christian unity?
The mid-twentieth century has found Christians of

178

many traditions trying out social and liturgical experiments to promote Christian unity. The agape meal has reappeared as one such effort. Some criticise this as a cheap option. It seems to circumvent rather than head into the sensitive issues of sacramental theology and ministry. Fully shared eucharist is the aim, they argue, and it can only follow resolution of thorny theological problems.

This may well be true. But sometimes we can only go forward by going around. Nothing would be lost and much gained if local Christians informally practised table fellowship and economic sharing. The striking features of the agape meal as practised among the earliest Christians are just as relevant today and are precisely the ones that could lead Christians into grassroots unity. Regrettably, we tend to remain within our own comfortable, inner circles of church life. It seems that Christian unity isn't important enough to us to arouse us to action. We are tentative, fearful or lazy.

Now as ever, *hospitality* is a highly valued Christian grace. *Redistribution* along biblical lines is equally timely. Acts chapter 4 records one of the first effects of the Pentecost experience among the new Christians. They learned to share *with thanksgiving* what God provided, and they found that indeed there were 'no poor among them' (Acts 4.34).

The meal we commemorate was a combination of religious and nonreligious acts. Prayers, hymns, biblical exhortation and thanksgiving for God's provision entered the context of friendship and conviviality. Surely this was the atmosphere in which Jesus' friends often joined him at table. And this is the setting in which we as disciples can meet each other and our neighbours. In this most vivid way we can remember Jesus' life, death and his presence among us. And we would begin to see Jesus' prayer answered: 'Father, may they be one.'

B.   The Peace

Remembering Jesus, being thankful, sharing hospitality, seeking unity and learning to share God's good gifts
– we have seen these themes recurring in the agape
meals from New Testament times onward. When
Christians' life and worship express all these things,
Jesus' prayer for unity is being fulfilled.

Reconciliation among people and between us and
God are central realities of Christian faith. It isn't
surprising, then, that from the earliest days, the
Christian Church made provision within worship for
expressing and effecting peace and unity.

The 'holy kiss' (Romans 16.16) was that provision for
expressing unity and peace. Christians adopted two
simple things – the everyday greeting of 'shalom'
(peace), and the embrace or kiss which accompanied it.
The way they incorporated these two things into their
worship invested them with more than ordinary
meanings. The everyday meanings – 'hello' and 'peace
to you' – deepened. These deeper meanings were what
made the kiss 'holy'. When, at the close of their
prayers, they exchanged the shalom greeting and the
embrace they were saying, 'God's peace among us
makes us one'.

It is obvious from the biblical allusions in the prayers
that accompanied the peace that they believed the Holy
Spirit effected peace. Sharing the bread and wine
celebrated Jesus' life and death. In a similar way the
kiss of peace celebrated the real presence of the Spirit
of Jesus among them. They believed that when they
were baptised, they were miraculously filled with the
spirit. In both Hebrew and Greek the words for breath
and Spirit are equivalents. Eastern people associated a
kiss with the breath of life. This made it easy for
Christians to interpret the liturgical kiss as an exchange
of the very breath and Spirit of God.

The kiss of peace (also called the holy kiss or simply

the peace) held a place in Christian worship from apostolic times and onward for several centuries. Special prayers accompanied it in the services. Unfortunately, after the fourth century, people forgot the kiss of peace and its true meaning.[31]

But here and there renewal groups rediscovered and used it again. Often this has been possible through the work of individuals or small groups searching for their radical Christian origins. In recent centuries scholars have discovered and translated into modern texts many writings from the early Church. On the basis of impressive scholarly work, the major liturgies have been revised in the light of the practices of the early churches. In these revisions the kiss of peace has reappeared in the communion services of many denominations, but its accompanying theology is sometimes left behind.

How easy it is to miss the full meaning of the peace. It can mean a casual 'Hello, how nice to see you' or it can even degenerate into a general brouhaha of hugging and chattering. But the peace can serve as a seal of love, mutuality and reconciliation among the people of God. The spirit among us makes our worship vital by expressing peace and effecting peace.

The following 'prayer before the peace' was translated into Greek from the ancient Syriac, a language closely related to the Aramaic which Jesus and his disciples spoke. Notice the connections between love, shalom, reconciliation, and worthiness to approach the table of the Lord.

O God and Owner-Master of all, lover of all people, finish the task of making us worthy, unworthy as we are, of this hour. Being made clean from every deception and from all play-acting, may we be united one to the other in the joining-fetters of shalom and love. Make us strong in the distinctiveness that comes from your wisdom.

Through your only begotten Son, our Lord and Liberator, Jesus Messiah, with whom you are praised, accompanied by your all-holy, good and life-giving spirit. Now and continually, and into the hidden times of the hidden times.[32]

These days, even in the revised communion services of the liturgical churches, the kiss of peace is usually seen as part of the preliminaries to the communion service. It is usually introduced with a simple and very old exchange of the shalom greeting, such as, 'The peace of the Lord be always with you.' 'And also with you!' The gesture of embrace varies according to the culture. In some places people bow, in other places they touch a cheek to the other's shoulder, shake hands or touch noses. They do whatever is simple and natural as a greeting in their culture.

Worship is not what special professional people do to us or for us, nor is it simply private devotional exercise. True Christian worship, in the Spirit's power, is characterised by remembering, by eucharist (thankfulness), by communion (sharing) and by reconciled unity. The kiss of peace expresses the reality of this reconciliation in our worship.

The kiss of peace would be equally appropriate in the simple agape service, and can serve – as it did for the earliest Christians – as the close or 'sealing' of the prayers, recognising the Spirit through whom they prayed.

In the kiss of peace we can say that relationships are right among ourselves and with God. When introducing the peace, early Christians frequently quoted Jesus' injunction, 'If you are offering your gift and remember that your brother has something against you, leave your gift there in front of the altar. First go and be reconciled to your brother; then come and offer your gift' (Matt. 5.23–4). They had caught Jesus' seriousness about the connection between reconciliation and worship.

It is important to make peace among ourselves, in order to enter truly into worship. Worship leaders can underline these meanings when introducing the peace in a service. Simple prayers for peace will help to deepen people's understanding and experience of the peace. They can read Scriptures on the themes of reconciliation, peace and unity in God's family. Here is a selection of texts about the reconciling activity of the spirit.

John 14.27 Peace I leave with you, my peace I give you . . .

Romans 14.19 Let us therefore make every effort to do what leads to peace and to mutual edification.

II Cor. 13.11 . . . listen to my appeal, be of one mind, live in peace . . .

Gal. 5.16,22,23,25 Live by the spirit. The fruit of the spirit is . . .

Eph. 2.14–8 . . . he himself is our peace . . . to reconcile . . .

Eph. 4.3 . . . unity of the Spirit in the bond of peace . . .

Eph. 6.23–4 peace, love, faith, grace

Phil. 4.8,9 . . . whatever is true, noble, pure, lovely . . . God of peace . . .

Col. 3.15 Let the peace of Christ dwell in your hearts . . . called to peace

II Thess. 3.16 . . . may the Lord of peace himself give you peace . . .

Heb. 13.20 . . . the God of peace who through the blood of the eternal covenant

C. Economic Sharing

Reconciliation and unity may well be gifts given to the Church, but we can frustrate the best that God has for us. The apostle Paul spoke to just such a situation in I Corinthians, chapter 11.

'Your meetings (for worship) do more harm than good,' says Paul (I Cor. 11.17). He understood that there would be no 'religious' unity without sharing of material necessities. Divisions between rich and poor humiliated the disadvantaged and undermined Christian fellowship.

The same often happens in our churches today. We do well to address the questions of economic sharing. We can work towards equality by changing outward and inward patterns. With a willingness to recognise need when we see it we will change our assumptions about hospitality, socialising and common work. When we are open to the intuitions given by the Spirit, listening, conversing and studying the Bible together, we will inwardly prepare ourselves to work towards economic justice within the church membership.

Out of a truly thankful spirit, material sharing can grow. In recognising God's generosity to us we are enabled to share generously with others. This sharing will spill out, not only to people in our most intimate groups, but into God's big world.

How can we express some of these insights about economics and sharing in our worship? Surely at the Eucharist (thanksgiving) and at the agape (love feast) services we should find a natural way to do so. When we are thankful and are responding to God's agape love toward us, we are poised with open hands to share our lives with each other and the world in 'communion'.

Jesus and his disciples gave to the needy around them from their common fund. So did the early Christians. And so do we today. Once a year many churches have a 'harvest' service in which they bring food and gifts-in-kind into a special service, bless them and distribute them to neighbours and needy folk outside the church fellowship. At Christmas-time some Christians wrap gifts for orphan children and place them around a tree set up in the front of the church.

This is good, but is there some way in which we could

bring giving which is economic re-equalisation more frequently into our worship services? Are there ways to integrate our sharing into the communion service itself? No other service of worship dramatises more powerfully our own reception of a gift from God. What would be more natural than to reach out immediately beyond ourselves to pass on the generosity we have received!

For Thought and Action

What similarities do you see between the agape meal and the communion service in your church?

Celebrate a *chaburah* supper in your house group.

Organise an agape meal in a neighbourhood group of Christians.[33]

Develop a Christian mealtime liturgy (similar to sabbath mealtime rituals) for your family, and invite the neighbours to join.

Incorporate economic sharing into your communion services. Symbols (clockface for time pledged, large purse for money shared, pictures or models of clothing, food and furniture available for distribution, etc.) could enliven the services.

Develop ways to include the children in planning, inviting guests, decorating table, serving an agape meal.

Introduce natural and non-threatening ways to express the peace of Christ in the agape or communion. Use a song, gestures, smiles, a Scripture verse or another symbol to show the reconciliation and unity of the church in the spirit.

8:   Blessing

Everybody has special words for parting company.
Many are rooted in a language from a distant past.
They often express the values and outlook of the
people. Goodbye is a shortening of 'God be with you'.
Farewell comes from a wish for good travel (literally,
'ford well'). The French put their friends in God's care
with 'adieu'. And millions of people in many countries
wish each other peace with modern offshoots of the
same root which gave us the biblical 'Shalom'. Whatever the words, the goodbyes serve as markers to end
the time spent together. They signal the beginning of
time apart.

Times together, like letters, need beginnings and
endings. If a letter's first page is missing, or if the writer
gave up in mid-thought and just stuffed it into an
envelope, the fragment isn't a satisfactory letter.
Similarly, an audience doesn't just straggle out of a
concert, getting up to leave whenever they feel like it.
There is a start and a stop to the concert, with clear
signals.

Christians come together for specific purposes at
particular times. The time they spend together has a
definite shape. It's different from time in a restaurant or
in a supermarket where people come and go con-
tinuously. Eaters and shoppers are a collection of
individuals bent on private enterprises. But in Christian
worship there is one deliberate purpose for being
together. This purpose needs to be indicated at the
beginning and ending of public worship. Hymns and
songs have clearly expressed Christians' intentions in

worship, as well as what they hope will flow out of their worship: 'We gather in your name to worship you' and 'Go in peace and God be with you'.

Very early Christians developed conventions and courtesies for beginning and ending their meetings. Sixteen of the New Testament letters begin with some variation of the phrase: 'Grace and peace to you from God our Father and the Lord Jesus Christ.' Scholars think that these phrases are evidence of set patterns in corporate worship which marked out the time when the letters were read aloud in the service.

And we can see that all the letters end with blessings and benedictions. But these endings weren't just signals to stop the meetings in the way that the school bell announces a change of classes. They were more than courteous goodbyes. They were genuine blessings, with significant meanings for Christians as they parted.

The God of Peace

> May God himself, the God of peace, sanctify you through and through. May your whole spirit, soul and body be kept blameless (I Thess. 5.23).

> May the God of peace . . . equip you with everything good for doing his will, and may he work in us what is pleasing to him . . . (Heb. 13.20,21).

The expression 'God of peace' recurs in New Testament benedictions. Surely its meaning is obvious. Isn't peace desirable and pleasant? Doesn't peace imply quiet, freedom from arguments and conflict, and toleration of each others' differences? Obviously God is in favour of peace. In fact, God is in charge of peace. How appropriate that God should ensure that we have a good measure of it.

But it isn't that simple. Peace is a biblical iceberg. Its apparent meaning may be true enough, but nine-tenths of its truth lies below the surface. We can search out the great bulk of its meanings from Genesis to

Revelation.[34]

The English word 'peace' is like an open door, admitting us into an enormous house full of blessing words. The biblical *shalom* and *eirene* in the original languages express the whole range of God's will and gifts for his people: healing, generous provision, safety, gladness, good relationships, life in tune with the natural world, forgiveness and salvation. These are only some of the many ideas that lie behind the words for peace in Old and New Testaments. Biblical peace means complete well-being. It means fullness of life.

Grace and Peace

Grace and peace be yours in abundance through the knowledge of God and of Jesus our Lord (II Pet. 1.2).

Mercy and peace and love be yours in abundance (Jude 2).

The grace of our Lord Jesus Christ be with your spirit (Gal. 6.18).

Grace, love and mercy are further words appearing in the benedictions which close the letters. All of them underline God's generosity towards us. 'Grace' is especially prominent. The Greek word behind our English 'grace', *charis*, simply means 'gift'. God's gift to us is expressed and mediated, through Jesus. His birth, life, ministry, death and resurrection are the supreme gifts (grace, *charis*) from God. Through them we can receive love and mercy, healing and salvation. The God of peace (*shalom, eirene*) is the giver of grace (*charis*). Those who receive the generous gift will be able to live in peace (*eirene*).

Grace is the gift. Peace is the outcome. In the Beatitudes, Jesus' word 'blessed' describes the life filled with such a grace-full peace. Blessed, happy, fulfilled are those who are able to live in humility and

188

meekness, craving justice. You are really living, Jesus told his disciples, when you live like this: when you are a reconciler, when you take the brunt of opposition, when you weep for the world. God's *charis* will enable us to live the Beatitude life. And that life is the life of biblical *peace*.

When we use these biblical benedictions, the expression 'God of peace' shimmers with the rainbow of meanings from the Scriptures. Going out from worship with shalom benedictions in our hearts can give us the basis for our engagement with the everyday world.

The rainbow of God's peace shines over the whole world. Shalom is not just for a privileged minority. This is clear in John chapter 20 verse 21, where Jesus couples the peace greeting 'Peace be with you!' with the 'mission' words 'As the Father sent me, so I am sending you.' The Father sent the Son into the world to reconcile, to save, to bring peace. And now Jesus was sending his disciples to carry on this mission. As disciples today, it is our job, our mission, to mediate that multicoloured peace to the people we connect with during the week. So the key words in our bedictions will be 'grace', 'peace' and 'mission'.

Non-Biblical Jewish Shalom Blessings

Grant peace, welfare, blessing, grace, loving kindness and mercy to us and to all Israel, your people. Bless us, O our Father, even all of us together, with the light of your countenance; for by the light of your countenance you have given to us, O Lord our God, the Law of life, loving kindness and righteousness, blessing, mercy, life and peace; and may it be good in your sight to bless your people Israel at all times and in every hour with our peace.[35]

Jewish people have always specialised in blessings and benedictions. The Bible is full of them. We must remember that almost all of the Scriptures were written down by Jews within Jewish experience and language. So why not look more closely into modern Jewish resources for additional prayers or blessings?

Surprise and pleasure awaits any Christian who spends even a few minutes paging through a Jewish prayer book. It all seems quite familiar, but has clear distinctiveness. Every page seems to burst out with thanks and praise to the un-nameable God who is also the God of many names. The blessed one, king, helper, saviour, shield.

Blessings and benedictions flower on every side, blessings especially upon God, the good one who does good. But also prayers of blessing on God's people like the one above. Notice that it begins and ends with reference to peace *(shalom)*.

> May there be abundant peace from heaven, and life for us and for all Israel; and say you all: Amen.
> May He who establishes peace in the heavens above, establish peace for all of us and for all Israel; and say you all: Amen.[36]

This example is the ending of a longer blessing that is prayed in every service of worship. The first sentence is said in Aramaic, and the second sentence, similar in meaning, is in Hebrew. Abundant 'peace' *(shelama* in Aramaic and *shalom* in Hebrew) is the shorthand for well-being on a cosmic scale, first on earth, then throughout all God's creation.

An old custom was for the worshipper to take three steps backward, bowing, as the second sentence was recited. This may reflect an even more ancient gesture in which the priests and Levites departed after the temple service. Where better to learn a *shalom* blessing than from the Jews themselves?

Selected Texts for Blessings (NIV)

Any of the following Scripture passages can serve as the basis for a benediction or a blessing. After each of the short texts is an example of a congregational congregational benediction based on the text.

1.   *Peace be with you! As the Father has sent me, I am sending you. And with that he breathed on them and said, 'Receive the Holy Spirit' (John 20.21–2). My peace I give you . . . Do not let your hearts be troubled and do not be afraid. (John 14.27).*

Leader: Jesus said: Peace is what I leave with
                                  you.
                                  Don't be worried and upset.
                                  Don't be afraid.
                                  My own peace is what I am
                                  giving to you.

ALL: LET US GO OUT IN THE SPIRIT OF JESUS. LET US
         GO OUT INTO HIS PEACE.

Two texts serve as the basis for the short phrases of this benediction. The words 'do not let your hearts be troubled' from the NIV have given way to the simpler 'don't be worried and upset' (TEV). Jesus' words 'I am sending you' and 'receive the spirit' are the basis for the response (*ALL*). But they appear in the form of a resolution to live the life of the spirit in peace.

2.   *The Kingdom of God is righteousness, peace and joy in the Holy Spirit. Anyone who serves Christ in this way is pleasing to God and approved by men. Let us therefore make every effort to do what leads to peace and to mutual edification (Romans 14.17–9).*

Leader:	Let us serve Christ.
ALL:	*We will seek justice.*
L:	Let us give honour to God.
ALL:	*We will pursue Shalom.*
L:	Let us be good neighbours.
ALL:	*We will live in the joy of the spirit!*

The leader speaks the three ideas in the second
sentence (serving Christ, honouring God, being approved by others). *ALL* express the three ideas of the first
sentence (righteousness which is justice, peace which is
shalom, and joy in the Holy Spirit).

3.   *May the God of hope fill you with all joy and peace
as you trust in him, so that you may overflow with hope
by the power of the Holy Spirit (Romans 15.13).*

> May God, the source of our hope,
> fill us, by means of our faith in him,
> with all joy and shalom.
> May our hope continue to grow
> by the power of the Holy Spirit,
> until we overflow with hope.

   The leader may read this blessing, or the congregation may read it in unison. It closely follows the ideas in
the text. The words 'our', 'us' and 'we' make the
blessing personal, and the effect is to increase anticipation of 'overflowing' hope.

4.   *He who supplies seed to the sower and bread for
food will also supply and increase your store of seed and
will enlarge the harvest of your righteousness (justice)
(II Cor. 9.10).*

> God, you provide seed for the sower
> and bread for food.
> You have promised both seed and harvest.

> Please plant the seed of your grace in our lives,

192

and make us to be fruitful in your harvest of justice.

We ask this for the sake of our Lord Jesus Christ.

Images of seed, fruitfulness, and harvest come from one verse of Scripture and are shaped into a simple version of the ancient form of a 'collect'. An assertion of what God is like, or what he does comes first. One petition follows and the short prayer closes with reference to Christ.

5. *Aim for perfection, listen to my appeal, be of one mind, live in peace. And the God of love and peace will be with you (II Cor. 13.11).*

Leader: Lord Jesus, show us the way to maturity.
Help us to agree together.
ALL: *The God of love is with us.*
L: Help us to live in peace.
ALL: *The God of peace is with us.*

Various translations give an array of words to choose from in writing this short closing prayer. 'The way to maturity' and 'agree together' are simpler ways to express 'perfection' and 'of one mind'. The congregation asserts the presence of God, who gives love and peace. Saying it themselves is stronger than passively hearing the ideas spoken by the leader.

6. *Live by the spirit.*
The fruit of the spirit is love, joy, peace, patience, kindness, goodness, faithfulness, gentleness and self-control.
Since we live by the spirit, let us keep in step with the spirit (Gal. 5.16,22,25).

Refrain: Let us live (let us live)
By the spirit (by the spirit).

>   Let us walk (let us walk)
>   In the light (in the light).

We will look at the world
   with love.
We will sing at our work
   with joy.
We will walk through the world
   in peace.   (Refrain)

We will wait for God
   with patience.
We will listen to others
   with kindness.
We will do our work
   with goodness.   (Refrain)

We will keep our promise
   in faithfulness.
We will serve our friends
   with gentleness.
We will speak the truth
   with self-control.   (Refrain)

Short rhythmic patterns in this setting of the fruit of the
Spirit suggest a musical chant-like treatment. Or it
could be done spoken (not sung) with delicate percussion.

7. *We are no longer . . . foreigners and aliens, but
fellow citizens with God's people and members of God's
household (Eph. 2.19).*

   *(Christ) himself is our peace, who has made (us) one
and has destroyed the barrier, the dividing wall of
hostility (Eph. 2.14).*

   *Through (Christ) we have access to the Father by one
spirit (Eph. 2.18).*

   And in him we are being built together to become a

dwelling in which God lives by his spirit (Eph. 2.22).

Section A: Lord Jesus, you yourself are our peace.
Section B: We are no longer foreigners and aliens.
A: You have made us one. You have torn down the barriers.
B: We are fellow citizens with God's people.
ALL: WE ARE MEMBERS OF GOD'S OWN HOUSEHOLD
  WE ARE ONE IN THE SPIRIT!

The congregation speaks here in two divisions (right side:left side; or men:women) and then joins together in the statement of unity. This would easily lead directly into singing a song or hymn celebrating unity in the spirit.

7. *Make every effort to keep the unity of the spirit through the bond of peace. There is one body and one spirit . . . one hope, one Lord, one faith, one baptism, one God and Father of all, who is over all and through all and in all. But to each of us grace has been given as Christ apportioned it (Eph. 4.3–7).*

Let us eagerly preserve the unity that the spirit is giving to us. For God has called us to a unity of hope, and to a unity of faith. And Christ has given us each our due portion of his bounty in grace. May God be glorified in the Church and in Christ Jesus, forever!

This combines a gentle injunction with a simple doxology to make an effective closing benediction, in which the people bless God after acknowledging his gifts to them.

9. *Rejoice in the Lord always . . . Let your gentleness be evident to all. Do not be anxious. By prayer with thanksgiving present your requests to God. And the*

195

peace of God, which transcends all understanding will guard your hearts and your minds in Christ Jesus (Phil. 4.7–9).

Go into the world in the shalom of God's grace. Go in gentleness and joy. May the Lord Jesus give you a spirit as thankful and generous as his own. May he protect your minds and give you the desire of your hearts. Go into the world in shalom!

The imperatives of the Scripture text give way to an expression more like a blessing than instruction. This would be appropriate as a blessing for a teacher to give to students at the end of a Bible-study session.

More texts to use for Blessings or Benedictions
Many short passages of Scripture, in addition to those illustrated so far, are suitable for blessings and benedictions. Some possibilities follow:

Col. 3.15–17; I Thess. 5.23,24,28; II Thess. 3.3,16,18; Heb. 13.20,21; Jude 24; Num. 6.24–7; Ps. 29.11; Ps. 85.8–13.

For Thought and Action

Observe the typical ways your worship services are closed.
Try for ways to make a service flow out into the everyday world.

Choose a 'goodbye' song or a 'shalom' song to end.
Visual image for goodbye – rainbow or sun of promise.
Set 'the grace' or 'great commission' to music.

Mission, power and peace are strong ideas for the end of a service. Call for commitment to prayer and action.

Develop Scriptural benedictions that tie directly into the themes of the sermon and prayers of the day.

Postscript

One generation will commend your works to another;
they will tell of your mighty acts.
They will celebrate your abundant goodness
and joyfully sing of your righteousness.
Psalm 145.4,7

Psalm 145 is the jewel of the collection. It spills over with biblical worship. What, in the end, is it all about? Worship is celebrating in the presence of God. It is joyfully telling the ongoing story of his justice and his goodness. And worship is a means of transmitting that story, of passing it on from one generation to another.

Ultimately the success of our worship will be determined by whether our children and God's widening family across time and space will remember the story of God and live according to his ways. When the Church is faithful, it sees its task as passing on – and continuing in its life – the story of God across the generations. When this happens it will be a cause of celebration and thanksgiving.

Thankfulness. It is a fruit of worship, but it is also a discipline. Thankfulness is something that we can learn. The Bible words that we have been looking at can help us practice it. With thankful hearts we can see and remember God's liberation and love. Our hearts, and the thankful, faithful lives that are expressions of them, will communicate to our children – and our friends.

And they in turn will tell their children.
They will put their trust in God

198

and will not forget his deeds.
Psalm 78.6,7

For the Lord is good
and his love endures forever
his faithfulness continues
through all generations!
Psalm 100.5

Notes

1 James D. Smart, *The Strange Silence of the Bible in the Church* (Philadelphia, The Westminster Press, 1970).

2 For a fuller development of some of these biblical themes, see Alan Kreider, *Journey Towards Holiness: A Way of Living for God's Nation* (Basingstoke, Marshall Pickering, 1986).

3 Kathryn Dobson, 'Too Matey By Half?' *Church Times* (8th January 1988), p.5.

4 The following paragraphs owe much to Andrew F. Walls, 'Culture and Coherence in Christian History,' *Evangelical Review of Theology,* 9 (1985), pp. 214–25.

5 Robert Banks, *Going to Church in the First Century,* second ed. (Paramatta. NSW, Australia, Hexagon Press, 1985).

6 See, for example, Ramsay MacMullen, *Christianising the Roman Empire* (New Haven, Yale University Press, 1984), chap. 10.

7 Hans Küng, *On Being a Christian* (London, Collins, 1977), p. 231.

8 Lesslie Newbigin, *Foolishness to the Greeks: The Gospel and Western Culture* (London, SPCK, 1986), pp. 18–9.

9 For a helpful introduction to Christian understanding of personality types, see W. Harold Grant, Magdala Thompson and Thomas E. Clarke, *From Image to Likeness: A Jungian Path in the Gospel Journey* (Ramsey, N.J., Paulist Press, 1983).

10 Dietrich Bonhoeffer, *Life Together* (London, SCM Press, 1954), p.44.

11 Everett Ferguson, *Early Christians Speak: Faith and Life in the First Three Centuries* (Austin, Texas, Sweet Publishing Co., 1971), p. 161.

12 Brother Robert, 'Music and Song at Taizé,' in Jacques Berthier, *Music from Taizé* (London, Collins Liturgical Publications, 1982), vii-viii.

13 Robert and Julia Banks, *The Home Church* (Sutherland, Australia, Albatross Books, 1986).

14 Justin Martyr, I *Apology*, 67.

15 Basil of Caesarea, 'The Liturgy of St Basil,' in R.C.D. Jasper and G.J. Cuming, eds., *Prayers of the Eucharist: Early and Reformed* (London, Collins, 1975), pp. 83–90.

16 Hippolytus, *Apostolic Tradition*, 9: Justin Martyr, 1 *Apology*, 67.

17 Tertullian, *On Prayer*, 10.

18 *Apostolic Constitutions*, 39.

19 *Odes of Solomon*. 16 (*Texts and Studies*, 8:3), reprinted in Ferguson, *Early Christians Speak*, p. 151.

20 *The Book of Common Prayer* (1662), Prayer 'for the whole state of Christ's Church militant here on earth'.

21 Richard Foster, *Celebration of Discipline* (London, Hodder & Stoughton, 1980), p.28.

22 Charles Elliott, *Praying the Kingdom: Towards a Political Spirituality* (London, Darton, Longman and Todd, 1985), p. 131–4.

23 Irina Ratushinskaya, 'The Colour of Hope,' *Observer*, 1 May 1988, p. 34.

24 John Gladwin, *God's People in God's World* (Leicester, Inter-Varsity Press, 1979), p. 157.

25 *Didache*, 8, 3.

26 Tertullian, *Apology*, 39, 16–8.

27 Hippolytus, *Apostolic Tradition, 25–7*.

28 *Didache*, 4, 8.

29 Hippolytus, *Apostolic Tradition*, 4.

30 *The Brethren Encyclopedia* (Philadelphia, The Brethren Encyclopedia, Inc., 1983), II, p. 763.

31 For a study of this practice throughout the history of Christian worship, see Eleanor Kreider, 'Let the Faithful Greet Each Other: The Kiss of Peace,' *Conrad Grebel Review*, 5, Part 1 (Winter 1987), pp. 29–49.

32 F. E. Brightman, *Liturgies Eastern and Western*, I (Oxford, 1896), p. 43 (translation by Jim Punton).

33 For a useful pack of materials to help you organise an early church love feast, see Eleanor Kreider, *Agape* (available from London Mennonite Centre, 14 Shepherds Hill, London N6 5AQ).

34 Perry Yoder, *Shalom: The Bible's Word for Salvation, Justice and Peace* (London, Hodder & Stoughton, 1989): Colin Marchant, *Shalom My Friends* (Basingstoke, Marshall Pickering, 1988).

35 *The Authorised Daily Prayer Book*, new edn. (London, Eyre and Spottiswoode Ltd, 1962), p. 306.

36 Chaim Raphael, ed., *A Jewish Book of Common Prayer* (London, Weidenfeld and Nicolson, 1985), p. 71.

Other Marshall Pickering Paperbacks

RICH IN FAITH

Colin Whittaker

Colin Whittaker's persuasive new book is written for ordinary people all of whom have access to faith, a source of pure gold even when miracles and healing seem to happen to other people only.

The author identifies ten specific ways to keep going on the road to faith-riches, starting where faith must always begin—with God himself, the Holy Spirit, the Bible, signs and wonders, evangelism, tongues and finally to eternal life with Christ.

OUR GOD IS GOOD

Yonggi Cho

This new book from Pastor Cho describes the blessings, spiritual and material, that reward the believer. Yonggi Cho presents his understanding of the fullness of salvation, bringing wholeness to God's people.

HEARTS AFLAME
Stories from the Church of Chile

Barbara Bazley

Hearts Aflame is a book suffused with love for the large, sometimes violent country of Chile and joy at the power of the Gospel taking root.

Each chapter is a story in itself, telling of some encounter, episode of friendship that has left its mark on the author's life.

THE PLIGHT OF MAN AND THE POWER OF GOD

Dr Martin Lloyd-Jones

The text of one of the highly esteemed sermons given by Dr Martin Lloyd-Jones, based on verses from Romans, Chapter One, focuses on our need to be entirely committed to the Christian gospel.

Dr Lloyd-Jones highlights the uniqueness of the faith. Because of this he stresses the necessity of our absolute commitment to Christ and his call to us.

This book will be of great interest to all thoughtful Christians and of help to preachers, speakers and students.

THE NATURAL TOUCH

Kim Swithinbank

Some people think of 'evangelism' as knocking on doors, reading your Bible on the train or starting up conversations with strangers in which you get on to the four-point-plan-of salvation as quickly as possible. Some of these activities we would do, others we'd cringe at doing.

In his first book, Kim Swithinbank says that sharing our hope in Christ is something that we are *all* asked to do. It should be as natural as breathing to us.

Taking us through the most common obstacles which keep people away from Christianity, he shows how we can develop a lifestyle which is attractive and compelling for Christ.

Kim Swithinbank is Director of Evangelism at All Souls, Langham Place.